All-New Edition

BRAIN GAMES

FOR

BRAIN POWER

MORE THAN 250 WORD GAMES, LOGIC PUZZLES, NUMBER CHALLENGES, AND TRIVIA QUIZZES

TRUSTED
MEDIA
BRANDS

New York / Montreal

Copyright © 2019 Trusted Media Brands, Inc.
ISBN 978-1-62145-469-4

Printed in China
10 9 8 7 6 5 4 3 2 1

Note to Readers
The consultants, writers, editors, and proofreaders have taken all reasonable measures
to confirm and verify the accuracy of the information contained in this title. However,
some statements of fact can be open to interpretation. Similarly, new information and
research often reveal that long-held beliefs are not true. We welcome your input on
any answers for which you have sound evidence may be incorrect.

STAY SHARP, STAY YOUNG

The puzzles in this book may help you improve a variety of brain skills, including your ability to remember. As the brain ages, vocabulary may remain strong, but the ability to spot meanings and search for the word you are looking for slows down.

Language puzzles exercise circuits that can help lessen forgetful moments and shorten their duration, but learning cannot become memory without concentration, and without regular maintenance, concentration shrinks with age. These puzzles provide many opportunities for improving and strengthening this important ability and many other useful brain skills:

• pattern and pathfinding puzzles will strengthen your powers of concentration in the same way that physical exercises build aerobic stamina;

• logic and memory puzzles will challenge your working memory because you must keep some variables in mind while you test them against others—this frontal-lobe skill is crucial to productive thinking and requires fierce concentration;

• visual and mechanical puzzles will stretch your visual-spatial mental muscles, which you need to navigate the physical world successfully;

• divergent thinking puzzles will encourage your ability to think "outside the box" and see links where others see standard differences—an ability that pays off in any profession;

• puzzles involving calculation are important to try—even if you are not a numbers person—for they light up many different parts of the brain at once.

Descriptions of the major puzzle types appear on the following pages. The puzzles and games start on page 8. Good luck!

About the Puzzles

Brain Games for Brain Power is filled with a delightful mix of classic and new puzzle types. To help you get started, here are instructions, tips, and some examples.

WORD GAMES

CROSSWORD PUZZLES

Clues are the deciding factor that determine crossword-solving difficulty. Many solvers mistakenly think strange and unusual words are what make a puzzle challenging. In reality, crossword constructors generally try to avoid grid esoterica, opting for familiar words and expressions.

WORD SUDOKU

The basic sudoku puzzle is a 9 x 9 square grid, split into nine square regions, each containing nine cells. You need to complete the grid so that each row, each column, and each 3 x 3 frame contains the nine letters from the black box above the grid.

There is always a hidden nine-letter word in the diagonal from top left to bottom right.

EXAMPLE	SOLUTION

WORD POWER

These multiple-choice quizzes test your knowledge of grammar and language and help you develop a better vocabulary. Find out where you stand on the Word Power scale by using the simple rating system included on the answer pages.

WORD SEARCHES

In a word search, the challenge is to find hidden words within a grid of letters. Words can be found in vertical columns or horizontal rows or along diagonals, with the letters of the words running either forward or backward.

NUMBER GAMES

SUDOKU

The basic sudoku puzzle is a 9 x 9 square grid, split into nine square regions, each containing nine cells. Complete the grid so that each row, each column, and each 3 x 3 frame contains every number from 1 to 9.

EXAMPLE	SOLUTION

In addition to classic sudoku puzzles, you'll find **SUDOKU X** puzzles, where the main diagonals must include every number from 1 to 9, and **SUDOKU TWINS,** with two overlapping grids.

KAKURO

These puzzles are like crosswords with numbers. There are clues across and down, but the clues are numbers. The solution is a sum that adds up to the clue number.

Each number in a black area is the sum of the numbers that you have to enter in the next empty boxes. The empty boxes that make up the sum are called a run. The sum of the across run is written above the diagonal in the black area, while the sum of the down run is written below the diagonal.

Runs must contain only the numbers 1 through 9, and each number in a run can be used only once. The gray boxes contain only odd numbers; the white contain only even numbers.

EXAMPLE   **SOLUTION**

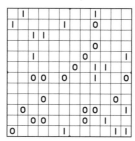

EXAMPLE

The odd puzzles feature an 11 x 11 grid. You need to complete the grid with zeros and ones until there are 5 zeros and 6 ones in every row and column.

KEEP GOING

In this puzzle, start on a blank square of your choice and connect as many blank squares as possible with one single continuous line.

You can only connect squares along vertical and horizontal lines, not along diagonals. You must continue the connecting line up until the next obstacle—i.e., the rim of the box, a black square, or a square that has already been used.

You can change direction at any obstacle you meet. Each square can be used only once. The number of blank squares left unused is marked in the upper square. There may be more than one solution, but we include only one solution in our answer key.

LOGIC PUZZLES

BINAIRO

Binairo puzzles look similar to sudoku puzzles. They are just as simple and challenging, but that is where the similarity ends.

There are two versions: odd and even. The even puzzles feature a 12 x 12 grid. You need to complete the grid with zeros and ones, until there are 6 zeros and 6 ones in every row and every column. No more than two of the same number can be next to or under each other. Rows or columns with exactly the same combination are not allowed.

EXAMPLE   **SOLUTION**

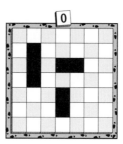
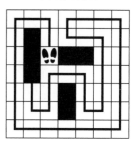

About the Puzzles *(continued)*

NUMBER CLUSTER

Number cluster puzzles are language-free, logical numerical problems. They consist of cubes on a 6 x 6 grid. Numbers have been placed in some of the cubes, while the rest are empty. Your challenge is to complete the grid by creating runs of the same number and length as the number supplied. So where a cube with the number 5 has been included on the grid, you need to create a run of five number 5's, including the cube already shown. The run can be horizontal, vertical, or both horizontal and vertical.

EXAMPLE   SOLUTION

WORD PYRAMID

Each word in the pyramid has the letters of the word above it, plus a new letter.

Using the clues given, answer No.1 and then work your way to the base of the pyramid to complete the word pyramid.

SPORT MAZE

This puzzle is presented on a 6 x 6 grid. Your starting point is indicated by a red cell with a ball and a number. Your objective is to draw the shortest route from the ball to the goal, the only square without a number. You can move only along vertical and horizontal lines, but not along diagonals. The figure on each square indicates the number of squares the ball must be moved in the same direction. You can change direction at each stop.

EXAMPLE   SOLUTION

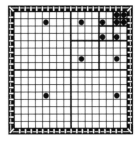

CAGE THE ANIMALS

This puzzle presents you with a zoo divided into a 16 x 16 grid. The different animals on the grid need to be separated. Draw lines that will completely divide up the grid into smaller squares, with exactly one animal per square.

EXAMPLE   SOLUTION

TRIVIA

TRIVIA QUIZZES & TRIVIAL PURSUITS

Trivia in a variety of formats and topics will probe the depth of your knowledge of facts. Questions and answers will tempt, tease, and tickle.

VISUAL PUZZLES

Throughout you will find unique mazes, visual conundrums, and other colorful challenges. Each comes with a new name and unique instructions. Our best advice? Patience and perseverance. Your eyes will need time to unravel the visual secrets.

BRAINSNACK® PUZZLES

To solve a BrainSnack® puzzle, you must think logically. You'll need to use one or several strategies to detect direction, differences, and/or similarities, associations, calculations, order, spatial insight, colors, quantities, and distances. A BrainSnack® ensures that all the brain's capacities are fully engaged. These are brain sports at their best!

WEATHER CHARTS

We all want to know the weather forecast, and here's your chance to figure it out! Arrows are scattered on a grid. Each arrow points toward a space where a weather symbol should be, but the symbols cannot be next to each other vertically, horizontally, or diagonally. A symbol cannot be placed on top of an arrow. You must determine where the symbols should be placed.

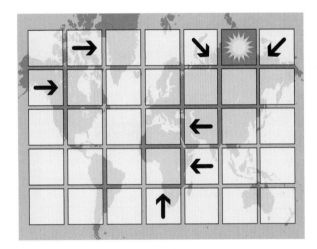

BRAINTEASERS

You'll also find short brainteasers scattered throughout these pages. These puzzles will give you a little light relief from the more intense puzzles while still challenging you.

CROSSWORD Fruit Punch

ACROSS

1 Rotisserie part
5 Pinheads
10 Gambol
14 Verdi opera
15 Acclimatize
16 Toledo's lake
17 Desire
18 Extortionist, e.g.
19 Ashen
20 Florida's spring training league
22 By and by
23 Horatian poems
24 Beatnik's "Got ya!"
26 *The Mask of Dimitrios* novelist
29 Franklin bills
33 Nancy of *Baywatch*
34 Stephen King's *Bag of ___*
35 Marceau character
36 Duck genus
37 Calyx part
38 Fashion designer Chanel
39 Nero's 98
40 Hectare's 2.47
41 Self-help book genre
42 Resort ENE of Tampa
44 Dickie feature
45 "Madcap Maxie" of boxing
46 Frigophobiac's fear
47 Hasn't ___ to stand on
49 Select carefully
55 *Rubber Soul* tune
56 Itchy
57 Petty in *Free Willy*
58 French 101 verb
59 Petting zoo favorite
60 Missing, militarily
61 During working hours
62 Alpine air
63 Real bore

DOWN

1 Did karaoke
2 Anchorage
3 Fresh thought
4 They croak when they get older
5 Don't agree
6 Extraordinary people
7 Ripsnorter
8 *Star Trek: TNG* empath
9 Lookout
10 Restore
11 Miami stadium
12 O'Shea in *Ulysses*
13 Ball-___ hammer
21 First lady's garden
25 Dentist
26 Be of value to
27 Fad
28 RIM smartphone
29 Had fingers crossed
30 Some, in Spain
31 Formal fiats
32 Animal's track
34 Swiss capital
37 Barely
38 "Clocks" group
40 Pub pint
41 Pious
43 "Hotel California" group
44 Ranch enclosure
46 ___ de menthe
47 On in years
48 Ford of The Runaways
50 Angelic circle
51 "Good grief!"
52 *The Music Man* setting
53 Grammy winner Sheryl
54 Potter's oven

8

Cage the Animals

Draw lines to completely divide up the grid into small squares, with exactly one animal per square. The squares should not overlap.

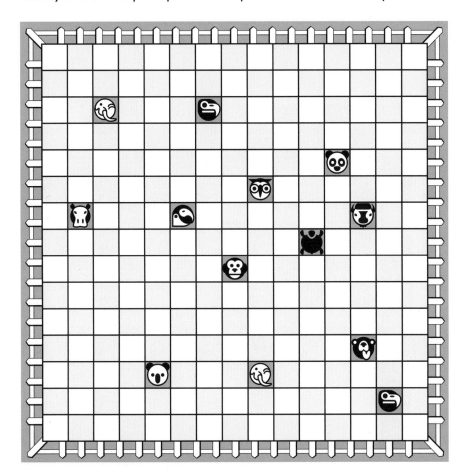

do you KNOW

What does your heart pump?

_____

_____

BLOCK ANAGRAM

Form the word that is described in the parentheses using the letters above the grid. Extra letters are already in the right place.

MINI MONT BLANC (outdoor sport)

		U									I			G

Hourglass

Starting in the middle, each word in the top half has the letters of the word below it, plus a new letter, and each word in the bottom half has the letters of the word above it, plus a new letter.

(1) Rodent
(2) Enclosed quarters that are forbidden to men
(3) Dishonor
(4) Similar
(5) Half
(6) Facial expression
(7) Not complicated
(8) Electrical discharge

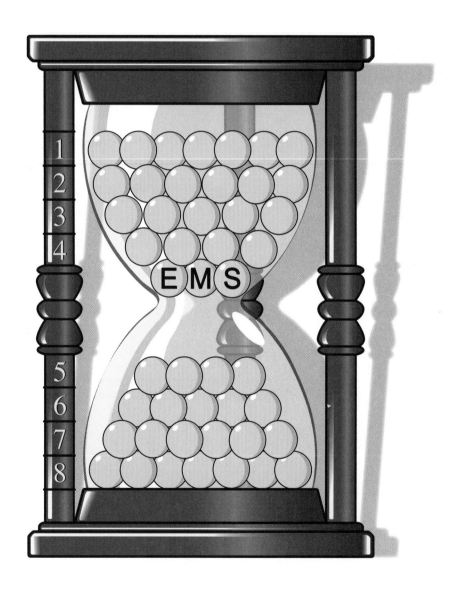

CROSSWORD ABBA Hits

ACROSS

1 Saw or wind ender
5 Go over big
10 Fish bait
14 Charles Lamb's nom de plume
15 Crow toe
16 Mrs. Charlie Chaplin
17 Sty cry
18 Christensen in *Traffic*
19 Perturbed state
20 ABBA song
22 Choral pieces
24 Action break
25 Currently
26 Plaza de la Revolución setting
29 Suffering
32 Stratosphere layer
33 Biospheres
34 Start of a series
35 Casino game
36 Having two feet
37 Cost of cards
38 "___ Blu Dipinto di Blu"
39 Makeup tool
40 Use a prayer rug
41 Canadian Arctic sights
43 Woodland gods
44 Hot, in a way
45 Feel
46 Like Oscar Night parties
48 ABBA song
52 Black, to bards
53 Immerse
55 Fork-tailed gull
56 Nickname for a slow person
57 Symbol on a one-way sign
58 Stonestreet of *Modern Family*
59 Cher's *Burlesque* role
60 Boxers' cries
61 1948 Hitchcock film

DOWN

1 *Cats* noise
2 Skating star Kulik
3 Scurge of serge
4 City between Tampa and Orlando
5 Designer McCartney
6 December air
7 Mingle-mangle
8 *M*A*S*H* soldier
9 Bewitched
10 *Fair Ball* author Bob
11 ABBA song
12 Component
13 Yoga class supplies
21 Mystic letter
23 They may be set in Vegas
25 Less likely to bite
26 Ex-Egyptian president Mubarak
27 Montezuma, for one
28 ABBA song
29 Expectations
30 Bury
31 Takes it all off
33 Dreary
36 Special occasion
37 Aardvark
39 Without
40 Madeline in *Blazing Saddles*
42 Creatures
43 Threaded fasteners
45 Phrygian fabulist
46 "___ we forget ..."
47 Proficient
48 Secure a flag
49 Roman emperor
50 Leaky faucet sound
51 Formerly
54 Hematite, e.g.

Verbs

All the words are hidden vertically, horizontally, or diagonally—in both directions. The letters that remain unused form a sentence from left to right.

```
A Y C R E A K V R E R R B P E
T L A O N G E K T E E H U Z E
R L M E D W I T N G P Y E T H
E U O X O R I T G I D E I S E
N B U E R S I A U I R N A G X
E B F C S J T L T F K H A T A
R E L U E S C E L L D R S P M
V C A T T A A A E N D R A D I
A P G E L O T R S E S N I I N
T B E V L S Y N N A I M D N E
E E E I A R E C T C O A B J K
E M C O T F C I S U M E K A M
O U B N E T S I L R P R M M D
W S S T C H E E R H O D L N E
H N J A B B E R B A H S I I S
I O N I A L P M O C S B F O F
Z C I G A M O D E L B M U R G
Z A S E C L I M B N T E N C E
```

- BIND
- BOAST
- BULLY
- CALVE
- CAMOUFLAGE
- CHEER
- CLIMB
- COMPLAIN
- CONSUME
- CREAK
- DO MAGIC
- DREAM
- DRILL
- DRINK
- ENDORSE
- ENERVATE
- EXAMINE
- EXECUTE
- FILM
- FREEZE
- GARDEN
- GRUMBLE
- JABBER
- LEARN
- LISTEN
- MAKE MUSIC
- PANIC
- REPEAT
- SHOP
- SHRINK
- STAGGER
- TIDY UP
- TINKLE
- WHIZZ

Keep Going

Start on a blank square of your choice and connect as many blank squares as possible with one single continuous line. You can only connect squares along vertical and horizontal lines, not along diagonal lines. You must continue the connecting line up until the next obstacle, i.e., the border of the box, a black square, or a square that has already been used. You can change direction at any obstacle you meet. Each square can only be used once. The number of blank squares that will be left unused is marked in the upper square. There is more than one solution. We only show one solution.

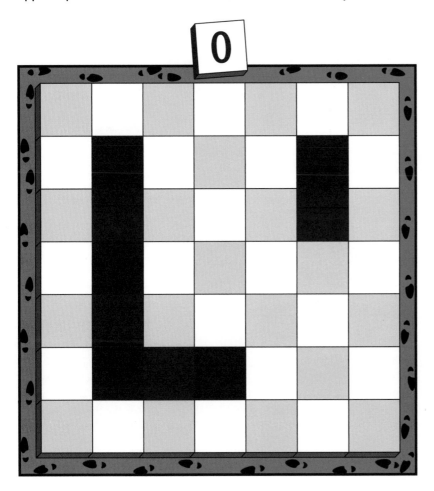

Popular Pets

ACROSS

1 Free ticket
5 Organ features
10 *Lost Horizon* guru
14 Bose of Bose Corp.
15 "___ Was a Lady" (1932 song)
16 Plane designer Sikorsky
17 Peace Nobelist Eisaku
18 Virgo's alpha star
19 Jockey's whip
20 Dr. Seuss book
23 At a previous time
24 Be obliged to
25 Picnic pest
26 Friml's *Donkey* ___
31 Moon's path
34 School group
35 Dirty double-crosser
36 Organic soil
37 Quit
38 Building by a barn
39 Alpine river
40 Miss Hawkins of Dogpatch
41 Lover boy
42 Scare
44 ___ *Mir Bist Du Schoen*
45 "Fat chance!"
46 Don
50 Ouida story
54 God or asteroid
55 Fragrant spring shrub
56 Made an advance
57 Blowgun ammo
58 River from the Savoy Alps
59 Irish language
60 BPOE members
61 Perk up
62 Neural network

DOWN

1 Hindu social class
2 City in Nebraska
3 Alma ___
4 Herald
5 Poem of six lines
6 Swinelike animal
7 Asgard god
8 Early Briton
9 Aquarium favorite
10 Moss
11 Indian tourist town
12 Disputable
13 Dada artist
21 "It ___ Necessarily So"
22 Mama llamas
26 Done in
27 Bed of roses
28 Covent Garden solo
29 Spanish surrealist
30 Town on the Thames
31 *Lemony Snicket* villain
32 Greeting from Simba
33 Naples neighbor
34 Give up land
37 Holy See religion
38 Ponzi schemer
40 Rug type
41 Penn in *Milk*
43 Pac-Man chasers
44 Stiff drink
46 Harsh light
47 Tractor name
48 Blofeld of Bond films
49 Perfumer Lauder
50 Asia's shrinking sea
51 Blockhead
52 Go angling
53 Skip town
54 Dutch city

MIND MAZE # Escape Plan

Hans the burglar entered the museum through the front door (A) and proceeded to the central atrium, where he took a statuette from its base. He made his escape through the open window (B) at the back of the building. Can you trace his route through the open doors from start to finish?

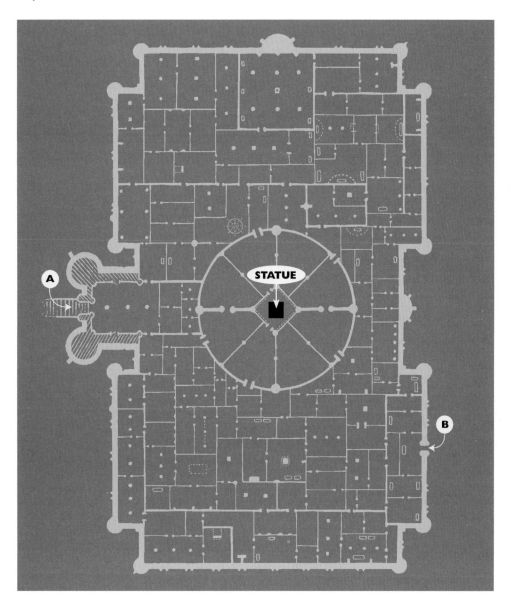

Sport Maze

Draw the shortest way from the ball to the goal. You can only move along vertical and horizontal lines, not along diagonal lines. The figure on each square indicates the number of squares the ball must be moved in the same direction. You can change direction at each stop.

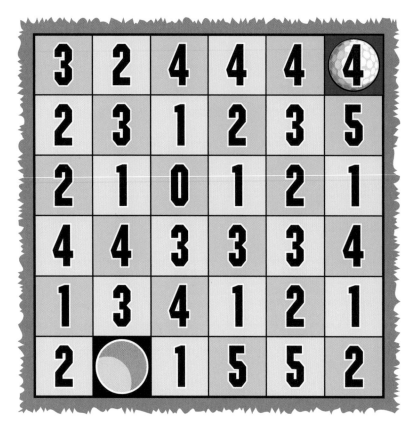

UNCANNY TURN

Rearrange the letters of the phrase below to form a cognate anagram, one that is related or connected in meaning to the original phrase. The answer can be one or more words.

BASIC

Word Sudoku

Complete the grid so that each row, each column, and each 3 x 3 frame contains the nine letters from the black box below. The hidden nine-letter word is in the diagonal from top left to bottom right.

	A E I N O Q R S T							

			N	I				
					T	A	Q	I
						Q		
Q	R		A		S			
	I	R		O				A
A		E		Q	T	I		O
N				I		A	S	E
					S			Q
S	R	A			N			

do you KNOW?

What is the word for a group of falcons?

_____

_____

LETTERBLOCKS

Move the letterblocks around so that words associated with biology are formed on the top and bottom rows. In one block, the letter from the top row has been switched with the letter from the bottom row.

A	Y	A	O	I	N	M
B	T	H	T	T	A	A

Spot the Differences

Find the nine differences in the image on the bottom right.

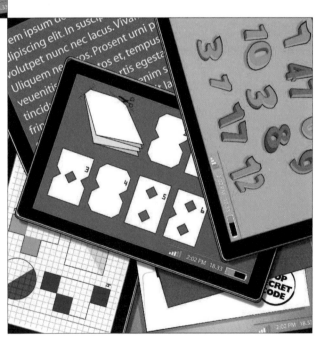

do you KNOW?

Which travels faster,
light or sound waves?

_____

_____

trivia

- What is the name of Barbie's boyfriend?

_____

CROSSWORD Checkmate!

ACROSS

1 Tabby's call
5 Cannes clerics
10 Sea-green
14 "___ said was ..."
15 Undergrowth
16 Legally invalid
17 Stallion shade
18 Deciduous tree
19 Hackman in *Runaway Jury*
20 Longest venomous snake
22 Pooch problem
23 It may be jotted
24 Argentine president (1974–76)
26 Keeps happening
29 Fondled
32 On the maternal side
33 Police shield
34 Mr. Iacocca
35 ___ of the D'Urbervilles
36 Sinks in the muck
37 Crichton's *Jurassic* ___
38 Sculptures and oils
39 Some sculptures
40 Fricke of country music
41 Giants
43 Collapsed in the clutch
44 Sister of Terpsichore
45 Sousaphone, for one
46 First month, alphabetically
48 History Channel reality show
53 Start up a computer
54 Stonehenge worshipper
55 Swedish furniture chain
56 Sites
57 Championship
58 Tiny bites
59 BPOE members
60 Dress down
61 Nephew of Cain

DOWN

1 Gospel author
2 Wellsian race
3 *The Good Earth* heroine
4 Hand-tighten fasteners
5 Monastery heads
6 Grease a palm
7 Raymond in *Rear Window*
8 Tomfoolery
9 "Mum's the word!"
10 Americans, south of the border
11 Brisbane locale
12 Forelimb bone
13 Pub brews
21 Reactor center
22 Out of the cage
25 10 million equal a joule
26 Put a new label on
27 Spanish year starter
28 *The Dead Zone* setting
29 Fruit vendors' stands
30 Creeptastic
31 Faked out, NHL-style
33 See
36 Jeff's tall pal
37 One of Rome's seven hills
39 Canaanite's deity
40 Monster.com listings
42 Optical inflammation
43 Supplied venture capital
45 Gabardine or serge e.g.
46 Up to snuff
47 Pocket billiards
49 Sonata, for one
50 Much in the same vein as
51 Auction vehicle, often
52 Fresh talk
54 Detox symptom

Alice in Wonderland

This year marks the 150th anniversary of Lewis Carroll's
Alice's Adventures in Wonderland. Carroll (aka Charles Lutwidge Dodgson)
invented words like *boojum* and *jabberwocky*, and his works abound with more terms
worth knowing. In celebration of *Alice,* here's a sampling.

. . . .

1. **hookah** ('hu-kuh) *n.*—A: staff of a shepherdess. B: chess queen's crown. C: smoking pipe.

2. **platitudes** ('pla-tih-tewds) *n.*— A: trite sayings. B: temperate climates. C: heaping servings.

3. **welter** ('wel-tur) *v.*—A: toss among waves. B: droop in the sun. C: shrink in size.

4. **lory** ('lor-ee) *n.*—A: tall tale. B: type of parrot. C: atmospheric phenomenon, as the northern lights.

5. **impertinent** (im-'pur-tuh-nunt) *adj.*—A: late for a meeting. B: talking rapidly. C: rude.

6. **languid** ('lan-gwed) *adj.*— A: speaking fluently. B: sluggish or weak. C: slightly tilted.

7. **ungainly** (un-'gayn-lee) *adj.*— A: not attractive. B: clumsy or awkward. C: sickly thin.

8. **livery** ('lih-vuh-ree) *n.*— A: model boat. B: uniform. C: long, boring speech.

9. **antipathies** (an-'tih-puh-thees) *n.*—A: miracle cures. B: sudden storms, usually in the tropics. C: feelings of dislike.

10. **will-o'-the-wisp** (will-uh-thuh-'wisp) *n.*—A: fast speaker. B: rare plant. C: misleading goal or hope.

11. **sally** ('sa-lee) *n.*—A: female rabbit. B: white smock or robe. C: witty remark.

12. **griffin** ('grih-fun) *n.*—A: monster with wings. B: horn. C: cranky man.

13. **cravat** (kruh-'vat) *n.*—A: game similar to croquet. B: scarf-like necktie. C: two-person rowboat.

14. **hansom** ('hant-sum) *n.*— A: horse-drawn carriage. B: knight or nobility. C: chimney flue.

15. **sagaciously** (suh-'gay-shus-lee) *adv.*—A: wisely. B: dimly or foolishly. C: ambitiously.

Sudoku

Fill in the grid so that each row, each column, and each 3 x 3 frame contains every number from 1 to 9.

8			6	7				
	4					1		5
		5			9	3		
	6				4	9		
1			5		8			4
		2	9				3	
		4	7			5		
7		6					4	
				8	2			6

do you KNOW?

Who developed the theory of relativity?

_____

_____

ONE LETTER LESS OR MORE

The word on the right side contains the letters of the word on the left side, plus or minus the letter in the middle. One letter is already in the right place.

B A C T E R I A -I ☐ ☐ ☐ A ☐ ☐

The Midas Touch

ACROSS

1 Grow friendly
5 Come in second at the track
10 Round top
14 *Class Reunion* novelist Jaffe
15 Sci-fi valet, maybe
16 Not have ___ to stand on
17 Prolific poet
18 Bathsheba's first mate
19 Young muchacho
20 Midas' favorite apple?
23 Rhodes locale
24 "Wonderful performance!"
25 Stewart or Steiger
26 Inhabit
31 Jacob wrestled one
34 Jai ___
35 "Golly!"
36 Midas' skydiving need?
40 ___ *tu* (Verdi aria)
41 Horned goddess
42 Detested
43 Adopted
46 Copy from a CD
47 Reindeer relative
48 Andes animal
52 Midas' dog?
58 Rapier relative
59 Where the eagle has landed
60 Little Dickens girl
61 What a stitch saves
62 Madea Simmons
63 Toledo's lake
64 Ravens or Orioles
65 Manicurist's board
66 Cannon in *Deathtrap*

DOWN

1 *Perry Mason* investigator
2 Gold medal, e.g.
3 Small lizard
4 Got off topic
5 Lopped off
6 ___ Voldemort
7 "___ Baby" (*Hair* song)
8 Furnace fuel
9 Lake Tana locale
10 Elton John song
11 Omnium-gatherum
12 Carte before the course
13 Star qualities?
21 Nice school?
22 Gulager in *McQ*
26 Mackinaw pattern
27 They're found in banks
28 Verge on
29 Bag with handles
30 Observed
31 *CIA Diary* author
32 Social standard
33 Silver-tongued
34 Altar locale
37 Sobriquet
38 Popular cook-off dish
39 Came to pass
44 Turn in for money
45 Ginger ___
46 Once in a blue moon
49 "And ___ fine fiddle had he ..."
50 Salsa legend Cruz
51 "Stormy Weather" composer
52 Bloke
53 Mayberry boy
54 Olin in *The Reader*
55 Paper measure
56 Kathryn of *Law & Order: CI*
57 Row or rank

WORD POWER # Ring the Changes

Rearrange the letters in each circle to find a word.

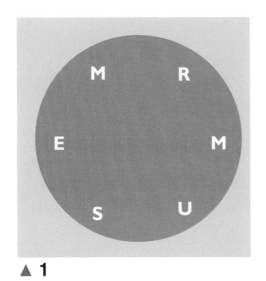

▲ 1

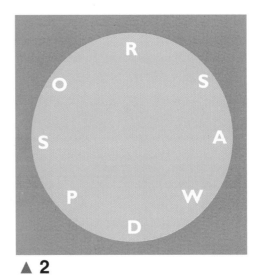

▲ 2

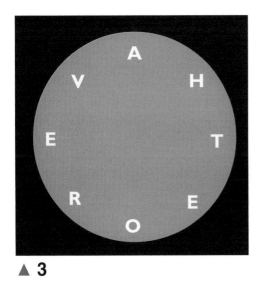

▲ 3

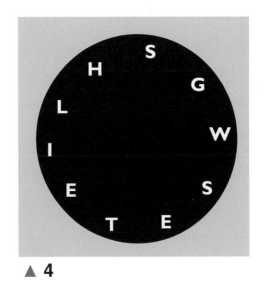

▲ 4

Horoscope

Fill in the grid so that every row, every column, and every frame of six boxes contains six different symbols: health, work, money, happiness, family, and love. Look at the row or column that corresponds with your sign of the zodiac and find out which of the six symbols are important for you today. The symbols appear in increasing order of importance (1–6). It's up to you to translate the meaning of each symbol to your specific situation.

do you KNOW?

Which is the nearest star?

_____

_____

UNCANNY TURN

Rearrange the letters of the phrase below to form a cognate anagram, one that is related or connected in meaning to the original phrase. The answer can be one or more words.

ONCE FRUIT

WORD SEARCH **Antiquity**

All the words are hidden vertically, horizontally, or diagonally—in both directions. The letters that remain unused form a sentence from left to right.

```
B A B Y L O N E G A H T R A C
A N T I Q U I T I Y S G E N E
P H I L O S O P H Y R T A A L
L E Y R I E O F E C R S L F T
S O R B T I D I M A R Y P E H
E P U U H C N P E E R I H U C
O N O T T I I A D S T H A D A
A O E E A S S I A T I B A B
E I G P H U R T S R N I E L N
T T N E E C T E O A E S T I S
P P W C M R I O T R L B T S L
Y I H T A O S I N I Y C I M A
G R E E C E R I H S L E I N V
E C E T R U S C A N N T I R E
H S O D A N T I Q U E H U C R
U N U M I S M A T I C S T I Y
N I O N O F P A P Y R U S W R
S I T E P I G R A P H Y I N G
```

- ALPHABET
- ANTIQUE
- ANUBIS
- BABYLON
- CAESAR
- CARTHAGE
- CELTS
- CHEOPS
- CHINA
- CLASSIC
- EGYPT
- EPIGRAPHY
- ETHIOPIA
- ETRUSCAN
- FEUDALISM
- GREECE
- HISTORY
- HUNS
- IBERIAN
- INCA
- INSCRIPTION
- LITERATURE
- MAURITANIA
- NUMISMATICS
- PAPYRUS
- PERSIA
- PHILOSOPHY
- PYRAMID
- ROME
- SLAVERY
- TEUTONS

Hello Spring

ACROSS

1. Poisonous snake from Africa
6. Airplane
9. Broadway singer Zadora
12. Word before flood warning
13. Large primate
14. ___ polloi (the masses)
15. Greek-American New Age instrumentalist
16. Opening ___ to let in the spring breeze
18. ___ Moines
20. Relating to birth
21. First day of spring
25. Golfer's goal: hole ___ (2 words)
26. Short hit in baseball
27. Smaller amount
29. Hisses, jeers
30. Corporation abbreviation
31. Tear down
35. Garfield's puppy pal
36. Paradise
37. Doctor
41. Spring bulb
43. Slanting
44. Sense of self
45. Break out lighter ___ in springtime
48. Speak without preparation (2 words)
52. Poetic word for unbolt (the door)
53. Tater ___
54. Tractor brand John ___
55. Scarlet
56. Double agent
57. Quench

DOWN

1. Spring month
2. Southern Hemisphere constellation
3. Males
4. Outlaws
5. E.T., for example
6. Bone in the head
7. ___ pen, used for allergic reactions
8. Sport with a fuzzy yellow ball
9. Picture
10. Someone from Dubuque
11. Row
17. Newsman Rather
19. Not a liquid or gas
21. ___ and flow
22. Status ___
23. Children's card game
24. Ohio city
28. Act I, ___ ii
31. Makeover for a house
32. *Much ___ About Nothing*
33. Meditation
34. Opposite WSW
35. Groups of eight
37. College student's declaration
38. Camp for troops (French word)
39. Chopped, cubed
40. Sort
42. Good heavens!
46. Cherry location
47. Pig's home
49. Actress Michele
50. Bother
51. Buzzy spring insect

WEATHER CHART **Sunny**

Where will the sun shine? With the knowledge that each arrow points to a place where a symbol should be, can you locate the sunny spots? The symbols cannot be next to each other, vertically, horizontally, or diagonally. A symbol cannot be placed on top of an arrow. We show one symbol.

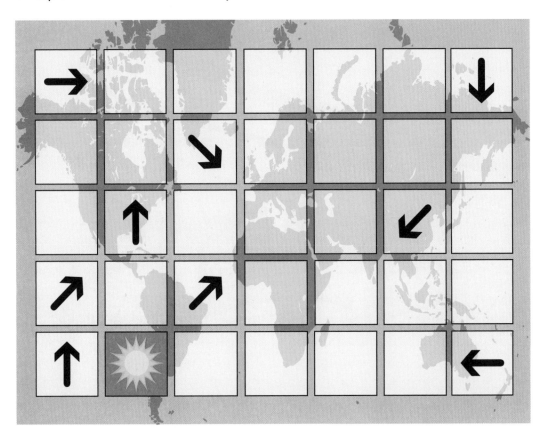

BLOCK ANAGRAM

Form the word that is described in the parentheses using the letters above the grid. Extra letters are already in the right place.

GUILLOTINE (fee for education)

C _ _ E _ _   T _ _ _ O _

Jump to It

Which number should replace the question mark?

DOODLE PUZZLE

A doodle puzzle is a combination of images, letters, and/or numbers that represent a word or a concept. If you cannot solve a doodle puzzle, do not look at the answer right away. Think hard—and outside the box.

CROSSWORD Daddy Ditties

ACROSS

1 Camp David Accords nation
6 Campus marching group
10 Square column
14 Innes of *The Event*
15 Sushi fish
16 Goggle-eye fish
17 1983 Michael Keaton film
18 Bond girl Hatcher
19 "Ooh ___!"
20 1986 Madonna hit
23 Sunday in "There Will Be Blood"
24 Pal of Larry and Curly
25 Fettuccine ___
29 Yokel
33 Agile mountain animals
34 Clear wrongs
36 Japanese caldera
37 None at all
38 Track prey
39 Gives a color treatment to
40 And so forth
41 Friend of Gandhi
42 *The Wreck of the Mary ___* (1959)
43 Considering that
45 Flabbergasted
47 Overhead rails
48 Jungle cuckoo
49 1954 Perry Como hit
57 "Oh dear!"
58 Émile Zola classic
59 Ominous card
61 Hawaiian goose
62 Speller's clarifying phrase
63 Troop's camping place
64 "Faint heart ___ won ...": Cervantes
65 Mother of Pollux
66 Doltish

DOWN

1 Stately tree
2 *The World According to ___* (1982)
3 Native Arizonan
4 Investment choice
5 South-of-the-border fare
6 Prefix for tiller
7 Sign word
8 Like sourballs
9 Striped squirrel
10 Zonked out
11 SEC overseer
12 Shower powder
13 Stage actress Menken
21 Performed
22 Eternal City
25 Chloë of Celtic Woman
26 Detest
27 Absurdity
28 "Gadzooks!" et al.
29 Hard pill to swallow
30 Lake Placid craft
31 River in France
32 Just beat (with "out")
35 Swabbie
38 Like corn and apples
39 Ravage
41 *The Haunting* heroine
42 Gave blood
44 Tom Clancy fan
46 Cheese go-with
49 Ivy League team, commonly
50 Tommie of the '69 Amazin' Mets
51 Shower-door piece
52 Ming Dynasty collectible
53 Dame Lyons of Australia
54 Yemeni capital
55 High-fiber cereal
56 Cry over spilled milk
60 Souvenir shirt

The Planet Suite

Here's a straightforward round that won't take you light-years to complete.

1. The orbit of which recently declassified planet takes it farthest from the sun?

_____

2. Which planet is named after the Roman god of the sea?

_____

3. In which year did man land on the moon?

_____

4. What name is given to the group of planets that orbit the sun?

_____

5. Which planet has prominent rings around it?

_____

6. Which planet is known as the Red Planet?

_____

7. Which planet is the brightest object in the sky after the sun and the moon?

_____

8. Which is the third planet from the sun?

_____

9. Rocks that fall from space and collide with Earth are known as what?

_____

10. Which is the hottest planet in our solar system?

_____

11. In the *Superman* series, in which city is *The Daily Planet* located?

_____

12 Which planet's moons are named mainly after characters from Shakespeare plays?

_____

13. Who composed *The Planets* suite?

_____

14. Who directed the 2001 remake of *Planet of the Apes*?

_____

15. Which is the second-largest planet in our solar system?

_____

16. From what are Saturn's rings made?

_____

17. Titan is a satellite of which planet?

_____

18. Who was the first man to walk on the moon?

_____

Sudoku Twin

Fill in the grid so that each row, each column, and each 3 x 3 frame contains every number from 1 to 9. A sudoku twin is two connected 9 x 9 sudokus.

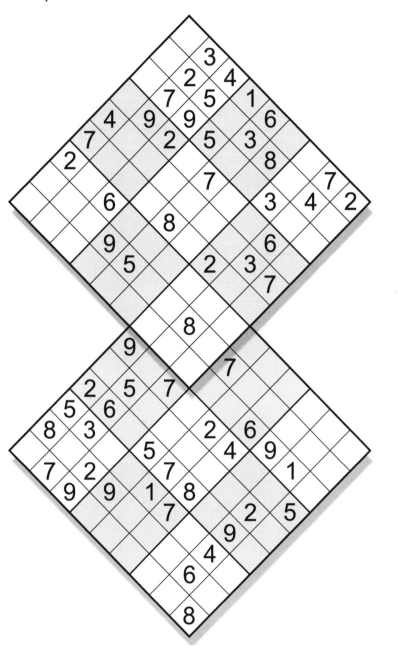

doubletalk

Homophones are words that share the same pronunciation, no matter how they are spelled. If they are spelled differently, then they are called heterographs.

Find heterographs meaning:

TO TOUCH ON A SUBJECT and **WORN WITH A PIN**

_____

_____

Word Pyramid

Each word in the pyramid has the letters of the word above it, plus a new letter.

C

(1) Electric current
(2) Curve
(3) Black-and-white whale
(4) Nocturnal insect
(5) Performed by a choir
(6) Intestinal infection caused by ingestion
(7) Academic degree

do you KNOW?

What is the name of Charlie Brown's dog?

_____

_____

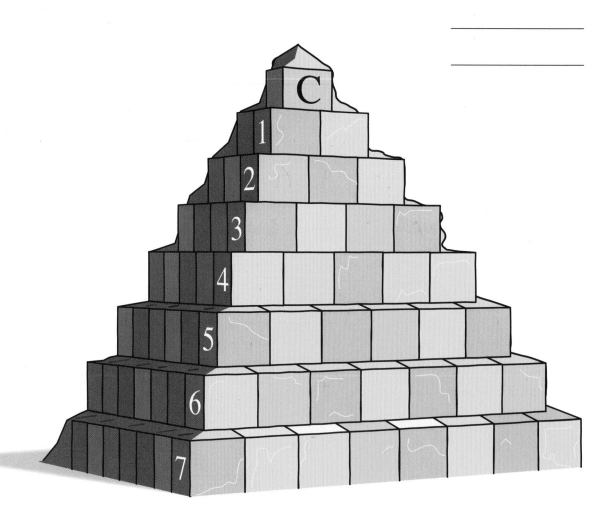

CROSSWORD Play Ball

ACROSS

1. Mrs. Gorbachev
6. Not many
9. Health club
12. Speak
13. Retirement plan
14. Pale
15. Gets close to
16. Baseball ___ average
18. Word with feather or constrictor
20. Painting setting
21. A baseball game has nine, usually
25. Clothing store Charlotte ___
26. Actress Delany
27. Lawyer (abbreviation)
29. "I'm an ___ book"
30. Wrath
31. God of love
35. Clothing closure
36. Colorful Indian dress
37. Diamond weight
41. One who stands at the mound in baseball
43. Got up
44. Homer Simpson expression
45. Warm-up area in baseball
48. Gave food to again
52. Lincoln nickname
53. School group
54. Forbidden
55. ___ Vegas
56. Infection site
57. Bee ___

DOWN

1. Score a home ___ in baseball
2. Dined
3. Call ___ day (2 words)
4. Certain Slavic person
5. Deliberate fire
6. Lie
7. Paleozoic ___
8. With too much liquid
9. Type of cheese or chocolate
10. Window glass sections
11. Corner
17. Letter after sigma
19. Once more
21. Wedding words
22. Siesta
23. Compass direction
24. Part of a purse, often
28. Lukewarm
31. Property that reverts to the state
32. Cheerleader's word
33. ___-Ida french fries
34. Address a gentleman
35. Treeless plain
37. Conspiracy group
38. Caribbean island
39. Parts
40. American Sign Language (abbreviation)
42. Civil wrongdoings
46. Airport stat
47. Neither fish ___ fowl
49. Govt. seekers
50. Long period of time
51. Classic baseball game food, hot ___

Keep Going

Start on a blank square of your choice and connect as many blank squares as possible with one single continuous line. You can only connect squares along vertical and horizontal lines, not along diagonal lines. You must continue the connecting line up until the next obstacle, i.e., the border of the box, a black square, or a square that has already been used. You can change direction at any obstacle you meet. Each square can only be used once. The number of blank squares that will be left unused is marked in the upper square. There is more than one solution. We only show one solution.

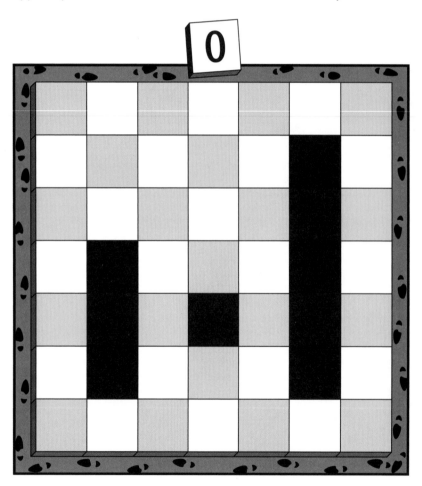

change ONE

Change one letter in each of these two words to form a common two-word phrase.

CROP CUT

WORD SEARCH **Space Travel**

All the words are hidden vertically, horizontally, or diagonally—in both directions. The letters that remain unused form a sentence from left to right.

```
I G R A V I T Y N A S W E R C
K C O D T H E S T A R D U S T
B E G I P C J M T C E J O R P
E L C R I C O U E N N I G N L
G O O F S S R L P P A C L E A
T B R V P N B H U I A V E E N
E L R H O B U S C M T S N I E
C N E A U Y A C H N B E N S T
N R T H B I A G E V U I R A O
E E D E S A A G U C C A A R I
I X E O R L I S E S M G L M D
C E P L I P S K U R A N U S B
S K Y L A B R U O G T I T T T
W A E O O A R I A N E S E R L
M O A P T S E R S R U O K O V
O E R A T A I K E E N R C N B
O Y T H E N U O N I T E O G D
N S T N E P T U N E A T R E S
```

- APOLLO
- ARIANE
- ARMSTRONG
- ATMOSPHERE
- BAIKONUR
- CIRCLE
- COLUMBIA
- CREW
- DOCK
- ENTERPRISE
- EXPLOSION
- GAGARIN
- GALILEO
- GLENN
- GRAVITY
- HUBBLE
- JUPITER
- LAUNCH
- MARS
- MOON
- NEPTUNE
- PLANETOID
- PROBE
- PROJECT
- ROCKET
- SATURN
- SCIENCE
- SKYLAB
- STARDUST
- URANUS
- VOYAGER

Sky Sights

ACROSS

1 ASAP in the OR
5 Still-hunt
10 Munsters' pet dragon
14 Woody's heir
15 Final strike
16 "See ya," in Sorrento
17 Blind, in falconry
18 Wear the crown
19 Industrial region of Germany
20 George Harrison song
23 Sitting on top of
24 Detroit union
25 Fruity quaff
26 Pedicab kin
31 HP tablet
34 Miss an easy putt
35 Heady brew
36 Moniker
37 Counterfeit
38 Judge the merits of
39 Sunlamp ray
40 Gettysburg general
41 Fabulous Greek
42 Hippie headwear
44 Atlanta station
45 Moose cousin
46 Catholic clerics
50 Infrequently
55 Use a harvester
56 Religion of Pakistan
57 *Time* 2005 Person of the Year
58 Window frame
59 Cameron's *Shrek* role
60 Villain's look
61 One-time orchard spray
62 Consumed
63 Australian salt lake

DOWN

1 2011 First Family member
2 Joyce Kilmer poem
3 Open-eyed
4 Brook
5 Moved with authority
6 Topic
7 "Video" singer India.___
8 Piano supports
9 Home of Mammoth Cave
10 Threaded bolts
11 Name of 12 popes
12 Waikiki locale
13 In tatters
21 Derby winner Funny ___
22 Cod relative
26 Valerie Harper series
27 Skye in *River's Edge*
28 2011 FedEx Cup winner
29 Countertenor
30 "Read 'em and ___"
31 Purposely ignore
32 Mauna Loa scoria
33 To ___ (everyone)
34 Honolulu-based detective
37 Whittling tool
38 Appear like
40 French Sudan, today
41 Anne Nichols hero
43 Farther down
44 Fair Deal proponent
46 Make smooth
47 Hog caller's cry
48 Copier cartridge
49 Snooze loudly
50 Killer whale
51 Patricia in *Hud*
52 Javier's home
53 Global land mass
54 Record blemish

 **Snow**

Which group of snow crystals (2–5) is incorrect?

REPOSITION PREPOSITION

Unscramble **ETCH TWO TRIPES** and find a three-word preposition.

_____

Word Sudoku

Complete the grid so that each row, each column, and each 3 x 3 frame contains the nine letters from the black box below. The hidden nine-letter word is in the diagonal from top left to bottom right.

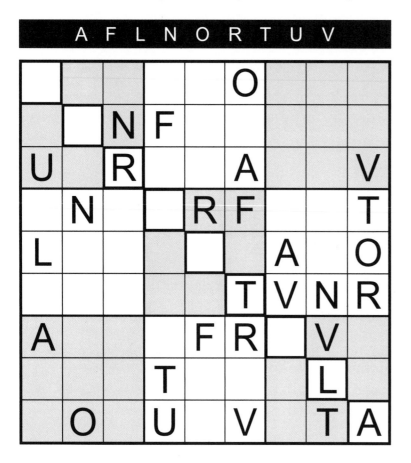

A F L N O R T U V

LETTERBLOCKS

Move the letterblocks around so that words associated with clothing are formed on the top and bottom rows.

I	N	G	N	A	L	G
A	G	D	L	E	S	S

CROSSWORD **Disaster Flicks**

ACROSS

1 Won't admit to
5 Language test
9 Word repeated in a Doris Day song
13 Sheltered
14 Musical group of nine
16 Rain pellets
17 Stocking stuffer?
18 Capital of Vietnam
19 Killer whale
20 1980 satirical disaster flick
22 Wobble
24 _____ and outs
25 Severe
26 Reverberated
30 French for without
31 Status _____
34 Imitates a leaky faucet
35 _____ Hawkins dance
36 Imposing vase
37 Papa's mate
38 Greek column
39 Bird's enclosure
40 Common conjunction
41 Finished
42 Los Angeles, CA, athlete
43 Understand
44 At a distance
45 Loving touch
46 Snouts
48 Derby or stovepipe
49 One on a stroll
51 The _____ Adventure, 1972 tidal wave flick
56 Praise
57 Care for the sick
59 Irritate
60 Has to do with (abbr.)
61 Muscat native
62 He was terrible
63 Stop or yield
64 Dictator Idi
65 Storage for jewels

DOWN

1 Immigration policy (abbr.)
2 Creatures from The Time Machine
3 Close
4 Shout
5 Available (2 wds.)
6 Types of horses
7 English queen in 1702
8 Lion constellation
9 Footwear
10 1974 disaster flick set in Los Angeles
11 Stir-fry starch
12 Winglike
15 1997 blockbuster set at sea in 1912
21 Avoids the truth
23 Celtic language
25 Models Gigi and Bella
26 Writers Ferber and St. Vincent Millay
27 Long-necked wading bird
28 1975 disaster flick about a dirigible, The _____
29 Greek exclamation
30 More reasonable
32 Prods
33 Whoppers
35 Coke and Pepsi
38 The Towering _____, 1974 disaster flick
39 Vehicle
41 Comfort
42 Belated
45 Milk protein
47 Bygone
48 Former Egyptian President Mubarak
49 Boxer Muhammad, Laila and family
50 _____-pedi
51 Baby buggy
52 Colored portion of the eye
53 Prima donna
54 St. _____ College, MN
55 Hawaiian bird
58 Actress Thurman

Sport Maze

Draw the shortest way from the ball to the goal. You can only move along vertical and horizontal lines, not along diagonal lines. The figure on each square indicates the number of squares the ball must be moved in the same direction. You can change direction at each stop.

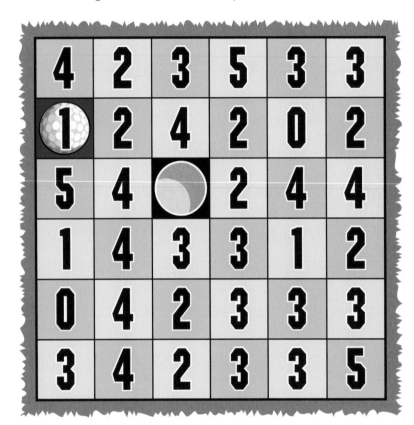

do you KNOW?

What is the last note on a piano keyboard?

_____

_____

Futoshiki

Fill in the 5 x 5 grid with the numbers from 1 to 5 once per row and column, while following the greater-than/lesser-than symbols shown. There is only one valid solution that can be reached through logic and clear thinking alone!

	1		4	
	<			
<			3	4
			<	
2	>		>	

(Column symbols: between row 2 and row 3, ∨ under cell 2 and ∧ under cell 3; between row 4 and row 5, ∨ under cell 2 and ∧ under cell 5)

trivia

- In what country did India ink originate?

_____

CONNECT TWO

An oxymoron is a combination of seemingly contradictory or incongruous words, such as "science fiction" (science means "knowledge or study dealing with facts or truth," while fiction means "an imagined or invented creation"). Connect the words with meanings that oppose each other and make oxymorons.

BONELESS	SHORTS
ALL	ESTIMATE
LONG	ALONE
FIRM	RIBS

Movies

ACROSS

1 South Sea isle
5 Big tooth
10 Cheerless
14 In the thick of
15 Weigh in
16 Blade
17 Singular
18 "Amazing" debunker
19 Snitched
20 2011 Woody Allen film
23 Refrain snippet
24 "___ need to explain?"
25 Tenor Pavarotti
29 Guys
33 Use the soapbox
34 Decathlete Thompson
36 Sheepish sound
37 SpongeBob's pet snail
38 Come again
39 Whip mark
40 Rescuer of Odysseus
41 Riga denizens
42 Comedienne Radner
43 Circle-drawing tool
45 Troublemaker
47 Commando weapon
48 Will Smith, to Willow
49 2011 Steve Carell film
58 City in Poland
59 Caesar's wear
60 Pop hero
61 Kapoor in *Slumdog Millionaire*
62 Make into law
63 Took a spill
64 Liver paste
65 Office staples
66 Life of Riley

DOWN

1 Lip protector
2 Mine, to Mimi
3 "Swedish Nightingale" Jenny
4 Kind of theft
5 Saddle horse
6 Bright aquarium fish
7 Dryer fluff
8 Don McLean's "___ Love You So"
9 Christmas lawn decoration
10 Item
11 Smell
12 Wrinkly tangelo
13 1981 Nicholson film
21 *Dies* ___ (Latin hymn)
22 Prefix for ester
25 Spock trademark
26 Heavenly prefix
27 Billiard shot
28 *Golden Boy* playwright
29 Five diamonds, to Annie Duke
30 Daggers in manuscripts
31 Mr. Magoo's nephew
32 Antichrist
35 Work on Broadway
38 Put up a fight
39 Safari subjects
41 Like malingerers
42 Ecstatic
44 Acrostic, for one
46 Commands
49 Give an ovation
50 *Five Women* author Jaffe
51 Mine access
52 Whistler's effort
53 Some, in Seville
54 Miner's tool
55 Concert halls
56 U. of Tennessee team
57 *Legally Blonde* heroine

Train Your Brain

Cool Eggs

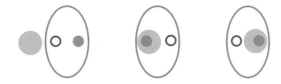

Which option below continues the above sequence?

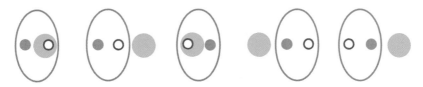

Designer Flag

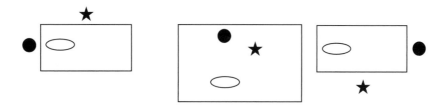

Which option below continues the above sequence?

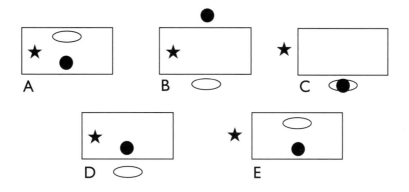

BRAINSNACK® Snakeskin

Which color (1-4) should replace the question mark?

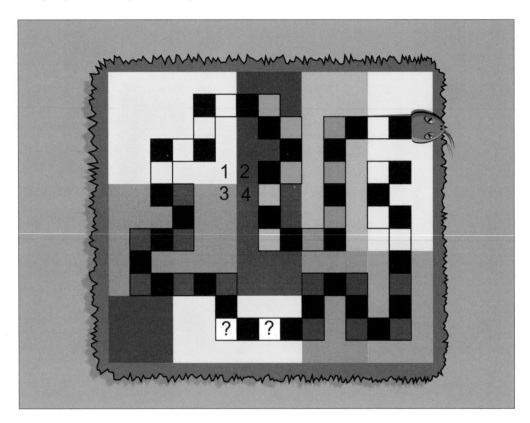

DOODLE PUZZLE

A doodle puzzle is a combination of images, letters, and/or numbers that represent a word or a concept. If you cannot solve a doodle puzzle, do not look at the answer right away. Think hard—and outside the box.

Sudoku

Fill in the grid so that each row, each column, and each 3 x 3 frame contains every number from 1 to 9.

1			3		7	4		
8		7			6	1		3
5			8			9		2
	4			6			7	
2		3			9			8
4		2	5			8		1
		1	9		2			6

do you KNOW?

What are tamales?

_____

_____

ONE LETTER LESS OR MORE

The word on the right side contains the letters of the word on the left side, plus or minus the letter in the middle. One letter is already in the right place.

G E N E R O U S -E   R

Look! Up in the sky! It's a bird! It's a plane! It's Superman! This strange visitor from another planet first appeared in Action Comics No. 1, published in 1938 by DC Comics. See what you remember about the Man of Steel.

FAR BEYOND MORTAL MEN

1 What were Superman's birth name and home planet?

_____

2 What was his secret identity on Earth?

_____

3 Name his adoptive parents and hometown.

_____

4 As an adult, where does Superman live and work?

_____

5 Who voiced the superhero on the 1940s radio show _The Adventures of Superman?_

_____

6 Who is Superman's love interest?

_____

7 Who were the newspaper editor and cub reporter introduced on that radio show?

_____

8 What substance lethal only to Superman was introduced on the show?

_____

9 Who played the lead role in the 1950s TV series _Adventures of Superman?_

_____

10 What Julliard-trained actor starred in 1978's _Superman?_

_____

11 Who composed the Superman score?

_____

12 Who created Superman?

_____

CROSSWORD Temperature Extremes

ACROSS

1 Present prettifiers
5 Conductor Sir Georg ___
10 Stereo's predecessor
14 Exercise aftermath
15 Beehive Stater
16 On ___ with (equal)
17 Stylish
18 Did some modeling
19 "Ooh ___!"
20 M*A*S*H nurse
23 Suffix for press
24 Oklahoma tribe
25 Web crawlers
29 Take a whack at
33 Diamond sides
34 ___ Haute, Indiana
36 Cars hit "You ___ the Girl"
37 Eagled a par-3 hole
38 "A ___ Day in London Town"
39 Lummox
40 Well-dressed fellow
41 Beatnik drum
42 To-do
43 Downright
45 Invalidate
47 Indian bean dish
48 Zippo
49 1995 Kate Beckinsale film
58 Kyrgyzstan border mountains
59 The Great ___ Pepper (1975)
60 Wished otherwise
61 Trig function
62 iPhone letters
63 Galena and limonite
64 Made a garden row
65 Ward off
66 Howling wind

DOWN

1 Fiddle Fugue composer
2 Eight, in Madrid
3 Iota
4 Out-of-the-way
5 Covered-dish ___
6 Great Plains Indians
7 Whip
8 Vincent van Gogh's brother
9 Diligence
10 Bad feeling
11 Moonfish
12 The Lion King character
13 Port in Algeria
21 Fits of rage
22 Tardy
25 Foul-up
26 Lace edging
27 Like Inspector Clouseau
28 Poker-faced
29 Vacuum tube filler
30 Aucklander, perhaps
31 Number on a liquor bottle
32 Soft fabric
35 Back to the ___ (Wings album)
38 Not a leader
39 Jeremiah of song
41 Bric-a-___
42 Fly like a moth
44 Swirled
46 Open a sleeping bag
49 Mazuma
50 Potpourri
51 Memory ___
52 Auntie of Broadway
53 Brouhaha
54 Garfield dog
55 Mystique
56 Film spool
57 Goods: Abbr.

MIND MAZE Treasure Island Express

Pirate Black Bart's treasure is buried on Deadlock Island. As usual, X marks the spot – but which one? Begin at the square containing the station. The word clue there will lead you to a picture answer in another square. Now destroy all the track in that square, and use the word clue in that square to find the next picture answer. Continue solving clues and destroying track until the trail of clues and answers runs out. Now return to the station and board the train. If you have destroyed the right bits of track, there will be only one X you can reach by train. And that's where the treasure is.

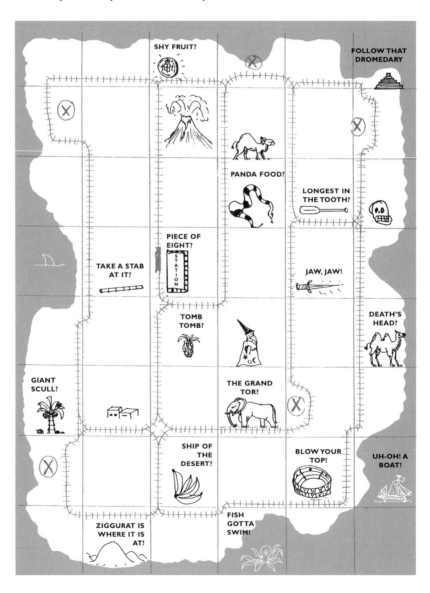

WORD SEARCH **Garden Variety**

All the words are hidden vertically, horizontally, or diagonally—
in both directions.

```
S C C S X L I O S T A A M V M S L I A
K M E S L Q E Y R E S R U N X G L H R
H I N M Y A A E K U N X O M A V G D F
O O H S U I U L D K W M E A T T D L Q
E W W L T L N N B A G W V F R J O X S
X I X A H U C R N T H F B E R W F P R
I H S I O B K H S A H S L R E W N V G
M H B N S H L E G O D L U R Z S X N F
X O U N E S E H N O I A S B I L V G M
Q N R E X D A Z I S K F Y P L A R N R
R U H R S I E Y T B D R Z F I T L A I
E M S E B P E S T N A L P J T N K Q Z
T E Q P J G B X U S O V U S R E R R M
A P X O Y S M X C M W A O U E M X E M
W K S T G N I D E E W P O B F A Y N A
V L C T D R V J Q O M K I Y E N M U E
J G K I S P A D E O K A Y F S R D R Y
Y A J N G R D T C T Q C L Z E O R P D
V D R G J Q T S E V O L G U D S D L C
```

- ANNUALS
- HOE
- PLANTS
- SHADE
- COMPOST
- HOSE
- POTTING
- SHRUBS
- CUTTINGS
- MULCH
- PRUNE
- SPADE
- FERTILIZER
- NURSERY
- RAKE
- TRELLIS
- FLOWERS
- ORNAMENTALS
- SEEDS
- WATER
- GLOVES
- PERENNIALS
- SOIL
- WEEDING

1950s No. 1 Hits

ACROSS

1 Carte du jour
5 Dances
10 Steel girder
14 Cat in *Peter and the Wolf*
15 *Adam Bede* novelist
16 Loch Ness Monster, for one
17 1955 Chuck Berry hit
19 Soccer's "Black Pearl"
20 Wouldn't take no for an answer
21 Where Mecca is
23 "...____ o'clock scholar"
24 Board for nails
25 Spake as a snake
28 Apple pastries
31 Pays a stud fee?
32 "Crazy" singer Patsy
33 Illumined
34 A ton
35 Street talk
36 Bridge coup
37 Touchy game
38 "____ Love": Brad Paisley
39 Assembly of witches
40 Least likely to forgive
42 Ohio city
43 House of Lords group
44 U. military group
45 Red-eyed polecat
47 Kangaroo and Kidd
51 *Winnie ____ Pu*
52 1955 hit by the Crew-Cuts
54 Tennis star Monfils
55 Mrs. Gorbachev
56 Skye in *Gas Food Lodging*
57 Weaver's reed
58 Noisy shoe
59 Racing team

DOWN

1 *La Bohème* heroine
2 Welsh form of John
3 Ayes' antitheses
4 Fair
5 Sang loudly (with "out")
6 *Annie Hall* director
7 Made stuff up
8 Either of the Chaneys
9 Hot under the collar
10 Disclose
11 1957 Everly Brothers hit
12 Gudrun's husband
13 Poseidon's mom
18 Will in *Blue Bloods*
22 Astrolabe plate
24 Brockovich et al.
25 "____ la vista, baby!"
26 Like Machu Picchu
27 1959 Lloyd Price hit
28 Lester of bluegrass
29 All worked up
30 Court employee
32 Mail grade
35 Tax reducers
36 Like cinder cones
38 Become sleepy
39 Terra ____
41 Hardly ever
42 Classy chapeau
44 *Midnight Cowboy* role
45 Newton fruits
46 Tel Aviv carrier
47 Place for corn
48 Frankenstein's assistant
49 Hawaiian goose
50 Killed
53 Small battery

Cage the Animals

Draw lines to completely divide up the grid into small squares, with exactly one animal per square. The squares should not overlap.

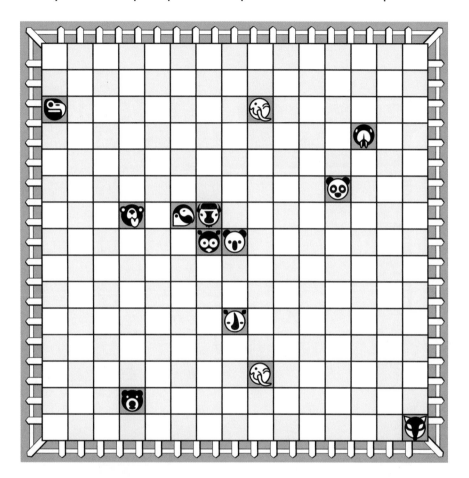

do you KNOW?

What is a vegan?

_____

_____

BLOCK ANAGRAM

Form the word that is described in the parentheses using the letters above the grid. Extra letters are already in the right place.

TEENAGE (hostile meeting of opposing forces)

| | | G | | | M | | N | |

Hourglass

Starting in the middle, each word in the top half has the letters of the word below it, plus a new letter, and each word in the bottom half has the letters of the word above it, plus a new letter.

(1) Relating to the central government of a federation
(2) Dreaded
(3) Dimmer
(4) Deprived of the sense of hearing
(5) Struggle
(6) Austrian who originated psychoanalysis
(7) Repay
(8) Beginner

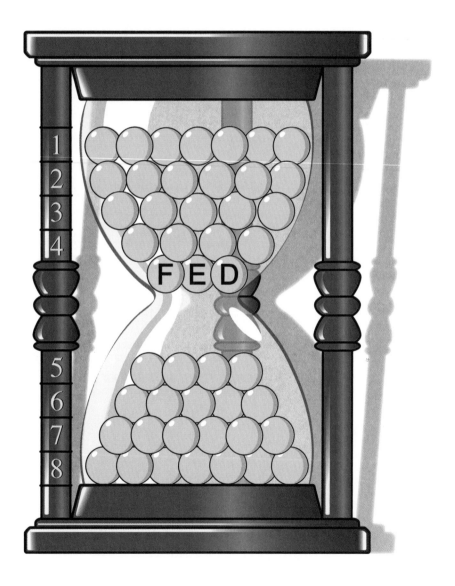

CROSSWORD **Punny and Funny 1**

ACROSS
1 Ho-hum
5 Golden Globes genre
10 "Hurting ___ Other": Carpenters
14 It conquers all
15 Try to disprove
16 Turkish biggie
17 Split into pieces
18 Make law
19 "___ and bear it"
20 How to race in the Rolex 24 at Daytona?
23 Tack item
24 Slap-happy stooge
25 ___ old how
26 Down payments
31 Driving problem
34 Country singer Travis
35 One who handles bookings?
36 ___-poly
37 Lines on leaves
38 Norm's wife on *Cheers*
39 Not lately
40 Garçon's counterpart
41 Halloween beverage
42 Like a roc
44 Bamboozles
45 Granola piece
46 Bulletins
50 Tennis ace?
55 It hangs out on the roof
56 Movie sections
57 Passions, to Pliny
58 Epiphanic cries
59 In a snit
60 Naldi of silent movies
61 Litter littlest
62 Play dough
63 Saintly

DOWN
1 Thespian Bernhardt
2 Alpha's opposite
3 Fishing boat device
4 Commonplace
5 White-tie
6 Gets a flat
7 Blind as ___
8 Considerably
9 Goes for
10 "Take It Easy" group
11 Soil: Comb. form
12 Trendy
13 Williams Jr. of Nashville
21 Honolulu Zoo bird
22 Rail family bird
26 Bore
27 Berlin article
28 Coated cupcakes
29 Rushed
30 Pull one's punches
31 Apothecary measure
32 Far from peppy
33 Zillions
34 Honduras port
37 Ford Crown ___
38 Calling on
40 Ferrari parent
41 Blanchett in *The Aviator*
43 "I kid you not"
44 Engine power, informally
46 Nick in *Hotel Rwanda*
47 Objet d'art
48 Poetic muse
49 Links legend Sam
50 Bottom-heavy fruit
51 Island near Kauai
52 Terrible czar
53 Lobby plant
54 Trig

Binairo

Complete the grid with zeros and ones until there are 6 zeros and 6 ones in every row and every column. No more than two of the same number can be next to or under each other. Rows or columns with exactly the same content are not allowed. There is only one valid solution.

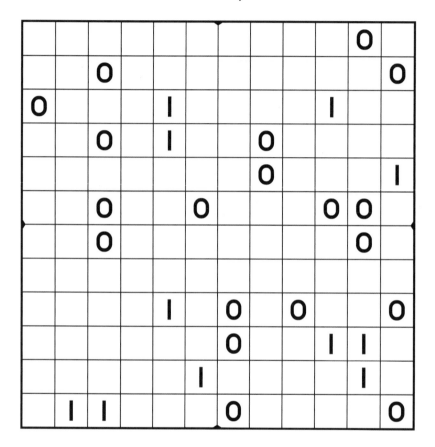

SANDWICH

What five-letter word belongs between the word at left and the word at right, so that the first and second word, and the second and third word, each form a common compound word or phrase?

B O D Y _ _ _ _ _ R A I L

BRAINSNACK® **Row Your Boat**

How many people are in one skiff?

DOODLE PUZZLE

A doodle puzzle is a combination of images, letters, and/or numbers that represent a word or a concept. If you cannot solve a doodle puzzle, do not look at the answer right away. Think hard—and outside the box.

On the Increase

ACROSS

 1 Extra dry
 5 Lute of India
10 Con ___ (vigorously)
14 Moore in *Ghost*
15 Looking down
16 Canal section
17 Yemen neighbor
18 Make shadowy
19 Virginia willow
20 Song from *Jersey Boys*
23 Curved bench
24 ___-di-dah
25 Hops oven
27 Galena, for one
31 Catkin
34 Applications
36 Penlight battery
37 More important matters
41 Meadow
42 Sicilian volcano
43 Bar mitzvah et al.
44 Sneaky maneuvers
47 Shove off
49 Previous to
50 Puget Sound seaport
54 Reality show with
   weigh-ins
60 Magazine section
61 Glacial spur
62 "Ob-___, Ob-La-Da":
   Beatles
63 God of love
64 Hands (out)
65 S-shaped molding
66 Kal of *House*
67 *Cleopatra* setting
68 Not a hologram, say

DOWN

 1 Acrobat maker
 2 Modify a soundtrack
 3 Spin doctor's product
 4 Doorbell ring
 5 Native Israelis
 6 Genesis victim
 7 Casting requirements?
 8 Augustan Age poet
 9 Total
10 Lighthearted
11 College drill team
12 Pastry specialist
13 "Fine by me"
21 Much more than miffed

22 Bert Bobbsey's twin
26 Decorative clusters
27 Rocky formations
28 Tom Sawyer's transport
29 Swiss river
30 Troubadour's tunes
31 Qualified
32 Conduct
33 Camelot oath
35 Impiety
38 Turncoat
39 *12 Angry Men* event
40 Mars black, e.g.
45 Like the phoenix
46 William Tell's home

48 Affirm to be true
51 Tributary of the
   Missouri
52 Jason's wife
53 *The Little Mermaid*
   character
54 Bend under a sink
55 Residence
56 Lord Wimsey's alma
   mater
57 Matey's libation
58 Hard to get hold of
59 Dance maneuver

Keep Going

Start on a blank square of your choice and connect as many blank squares as possible with one single continuous line. You can only connect squares along vertical and horizontal lines, not along diagonal lines. You must continue the connecting line up until the next obstacle, i.e., the border of the box, a black square, or a square that has already been used. You can change direction at any obstacle you meet. Each square can only be used once. The number of blank squares that will be left unused is marked in the upper square. There is more than one solution. We only show one solution.

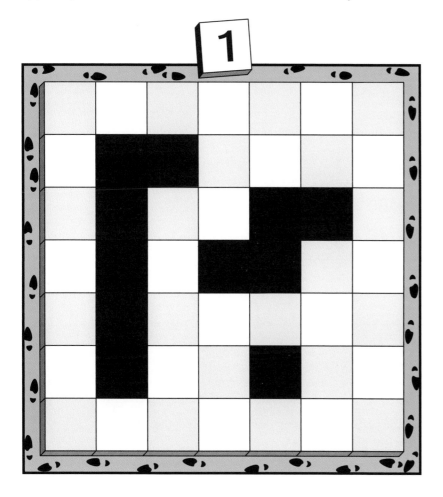

WEATHER CHART — Sunny

Where will the sun shine? With the knowledge that each arrow points to a place where a symbol should be, can you locate the sunny spots? The symbols cannot be next to each other, vertically, horizontally, or diagonally. A symbol cannot be placed on top of an arrow. We show one symbol.

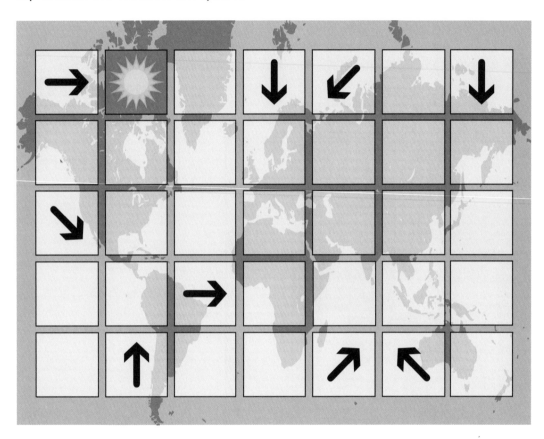

BLOCK ANAGRAM

Form the word that is described in the parentheses using the letters above the grid. Extra letters are already in the right place.

HERNIA (cyclone)

	U		R		C			

CROSSWORD # Pretty Beat-Up

ACROSS

1. Sackcloth material
5. Scruggs' bluegrass partner
10. Tag with a PG, e.g.
14. Eternally
15. Kind of show
16. Utilizer
17. Stand up
18. *Absolutely Fabulous* character
19. Visited
20. Maryland state flowers
23. Lemon of *30 Rock*
24. U.S. Open entrant
25. Italian toast
28. Uncredited credit, in quotes
30. Muppet eagle
33. It may be humble
34. Melville romance
35. Stadium audience participation
36. Elite study group
39. Exercise routine count
40. Baby bottle contents
41. Inventor Ampere
42. "___ he drove out of sight ..."
43. Mention in support, as a case
44. Enkindle
45. Portray
46. Teachers' org.
47. Pretty beat up
56. Biblical shipbuilder
57. Shire in *Rocky*
58. Tupper of Tupperware
59. Cube maker Rubik
60. Plain to see
61. Historians' study
62. Pal of wash
63. Dodger of Cooperstown
64. Garage event

DOWN

1. Coriander, e.g.
2. It isn't good
3. Badlands rise
4. Thwarts
5. Immobilize
6. Pink ___ cocktail
7. Indy speedster Luyendyk
8. See to
9. Measured dose
10. Rene in *Big Trouble*
11. Clueless
12. *High School Musical* extra
13. Diving eagles
21. Forged check passer
22. Capacious vase
25. British cavalry sword
26. More talented
27. Watchmaker's aid
28. Unhurried walk
29. Barnes & Noble tablet
30. Freeman or Patty
31. Duck
32. Saloon brawl
34. Death notice
35. Hopefuls
37. Rich Little, for one
38. Called by loudspeaker
43. A quarter of M
44. Inherent
45. Antonym for adore
47. From scratch
48. Collective wisdom
49. Turner in *Madame X*
50. Spelunking site
51. "Death and Fire" artist Paul
52. Don't put these on!
53. "Tomb Raider" heroine
54. River of Europe and Asia
55. The other thing

Actresses

All the words are hidden vertically, horizontally, or diagonally—in both directions. The letters that remain unused form a sentence from left to right.

```
O A N A C D Z T H E P B U R N
B R E S S N P E F R W O G T
R F O R I M H A E S O B I R O
A N A E T U H I L R E N N E D
G E W A P E F K R R T A O B R
R H I P O F E A T C A M T D A
A T E R E C F S A D L G S L B
F R N R A E P E A I E R I O R
T O Q P F O R R R E V E N G M
M W S U A N T T C T U B A E O
R Y C T E C N O S R E D N A T
I A H N E T A F W I N S L E T
I H N L W R T T L C E M E O E
F N E A T E U E L H D H S V C
O O I R M R A A O S A A O C W
N A D R N D T V R Y O O L N A
D C E E H A I W E L C H C R F
A A R C T E R K N R O L Y A T
```

- ANDERSON
- ANISTON
- ARQUETTE
- BARDOT
- BERGMAN
- CLOSE
- DENEUVE
- DIETRICH
- ELECTRA
- FARROW
- FAWCETT
- FONDA
- FOSTER
- GARBO
- GARLAND
- GOLDBERG
- HAYEK
- HAYWORTH
- HEPBURN
- HUPPERT
- KIDMAN
- LOREN
- MONROE
- PFEIFFER
- ROBERTS
- SCHNEIDER
- SPACEK
- STREEP
- TAYLOR
- TURNER
- WEAVER
- WEISZ
- WELCH
- WINSLET

Sport Maze

Draw the shortest way from the ball to the goal. You can only move along vertical and horizontal lines, not along diagonal lines. The figure on each square indicates the number of squares the ball must be moved in the same direction. You can change direction at each stop.

2	2	1	2	1	1
3	3	1	2	3	1
3	1	2	1	3	4
5	3	1	0	3	2
1	3	3	◯	3	4
0	1	1	1	4	4

do you KNOW?

Where would you find a cornea?

_____

_____

UNCANNY TURN

Rearrange the letters of the phrase below to form a cognate anagram, one that is related or connected in meaning to the original phrase. The answer can be one or more words.

TRY POE

Tee for Two

ACROSS

1 Falling-out
5 Mold or fashion
10 All-purpose trucks
14 Matty who hit .342 in 1966
15 DNA shape
16 Showering state
17 Money of Yemen
18 Put in office
19 Marathoner Zátopek
20 Yarn
22 Pottery glaze
24 Kennel guest
25 Optimistic
26 Lawyer's case
30 Stroller occupant
33 Poppin' Fresh is this
34 It calls for a blessing
36 Krupp of the NHL
37 Additional
38 Sweet ___ College
39 Rob Reiner's alma mater
40 Sign a contract
41 Disney film set in China
42 Cross-examiner, e.g.
43 Links reservation
45 General pardon
47 Shaggy Tibetans
48 Financial assistance
49 Half a rack
51 Beat a hasty retreat
56 Pressing
57 Suffix with fraud
59 Ballerina Spessivtzeva
60 Soon enough
61 Like a flophouse
62 Godsend
63 Groening or Dillon
64 Medal of ___
65 "Pushover" singer James

DOWN

1 Mouth-puckering
2 Skating star Kulik
3 Stud farm arrival
4 Newspaper ad type
5 Scabbard
6 Dante's inferno
7 Opposite the wind
8 Movie, slangily
9 Outside
10 Nervous
11 Flatteners of spare tires
12 Falco in The Sopranos
13 Liquidate
21 NASDAQ sector
23 A don't
26 Be a doorman
27 Hundred ___ (long odds)
28 Ragtime dance
29 NFL Hall-of-Famer Neale
30 "... faster ___ speeding bullet"
31 Baby who doesn't sleep at night?
32 About to cry
35 Leon Panetta's org.
38 Bouncer specialty
39 Was
41 Masters winner Weir
42 Has ___ (knows somebody)
44 Aptitude
46 Saint Stephen, e.g.
49 Man not born of woman
50 Black Swan heroine
51 Not Another ___ Movie (2001)
52 Nullify
53 Rafts
54 "___ the Sun in the Morning"
55 Turner in Peyton Place
58 Durocher of baseball

TRIVIA QUIZ **A Round of Golf**

Are you up for playing with the pros?
Before you step on the green, see if you can unravel this golfing terminology.

1. What nickname is given to the clubhouse on a golf course?

   _____

2. How many shots under par is a birdie?

   _____

3. On a golf course, what do the initials GUR stand for?

   _____

4. What name is given to the closely mown section of a golf hole between the green and the tee?

   _____

5. What is the American term for what the British call a bunker?

   _____

6. What is happening to a golfer who is suffering from "the yips"?

   _____

7. Name the royal and ancient club that is known as the "home of golf."

   _____

8. Which form of golf is based on holes won, lost, and halved, as opposed to the total strokes taken?

   _____

9. What do you call the person who carries a golfer's clubs?

   _____

10. Which playing card is the alternative name for a hole in one?

   _____

11. What name is given to a shot that misses the ball completely but counts as a shot?

   _____

12. What is it called when a player scores an eight on a hole?

   _____

triVia • The word golf likely originated from what Medieval Dutch word that meant "club"?

_____

Hamilton Lingo

The Broadway smash musical *Hamilton* by Lin-Manuel Miranda features
a hip-hop libretto packed with rich vocabulary.
Here are some words to know before seeing the historical show.

· ·

1. **manumission** (man-yoo-'mih-shin)
   n.—A: spy operation. B: the act of
   freeing from slavery. C: handiwork.

2. **complicit** (kom-'plih-siht) *adj.*— A:
   elaborate. B: in total agreement.
   C: associating with or participating
   in.

3. **equivocate** (ih-'kwih-vuh-kayt)
   v.—A: waffle. B: share evenly.
   C: tremble.

4. **enterprising** ('ehn-ter-pry-zing)
   adj.—A: go-getting. B: trespassing.
   C: just beginning.

5. **homilies** ('hah-muh-leez) *n.*—
   A: family relations. B: sermons.
   C: opposites.

6. **venerated** ('veh-nuh-ray-ted)
   adj.—A: exhausted. B: honored.
   C: pardoned.

7. **restitution** (res-tih-'too-shuhn)
   n.—A: truce. B: imprisonment.
   C: amends.

8. **dissidents** ('diss-ih-dihnts) *n.*—
   A: dissenters. B: immigrants.
   C: tossers of insults.

9. **obfuscates** ('ahb-fuh-skayts) *v.*—
   A: substitutes. B: glides gracefully.
   C: confuses.

10. **jettison** ('jeh-tih-sen) *v.*—A: turn
    black. B: rise rapidly. C: throw
    away.

11. **intemperate** (ihn-'tem-puh-riht)
    adj.—A: permanent. B: hard to
    resist. C: unrestrained.

12. **vacuous** ('va-kew-uhs) *adj.*—
    A: empty or blank. B: gusting.
    C: immune.

13. **intransigent** (ihn-'tran-zih-jent)
    adj.—A: stubborn. B: revolting.
    C: on the move.

14. **inimitable** (ihn-'ih-mih-tuh-buhl)
    adj.—A: incomparable or unrivaled.
    B: undivided. C: countless.

15. **disparage** (di-'spar-ij) *v.*—
    A: scatter. B: speak ill of.
    C: fire, as cannons.

BRAINSNACK® **Recycler**

With which recycling logo (A-F) can you make this pattern?

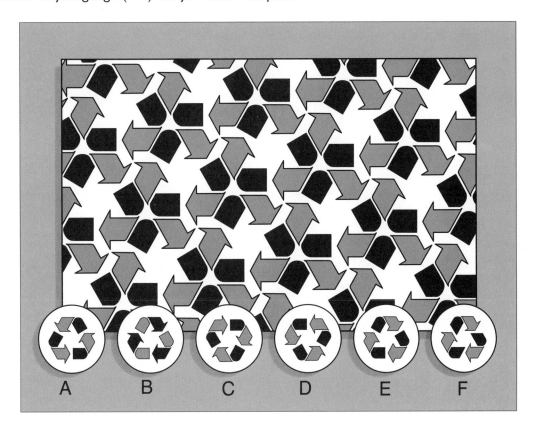

DOODLE PUZZLE

A doodle puzzle is a combination of images, letters, and/or numbers that represent a word or a concept. If you cannot solve a doodle puzzle, do not look at the answer right away. Think hard—and outside the box.

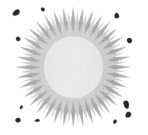

Spot the Differences

Find the nine differences in the image on the bottom right.

do you KNOW?

How did
Al Capone die?

_____

_____

trivia

• What was the name of the captain
of the ship *Pequod*?

_____

66

Sudoku X

Fill in the grid so that each row, each column, and each 3 x 3 frame contains every number from 1 to 9. The two main diagonals of the grid also contain every number from 1 to 9.

					8			
	1		7		5			6
	8	7						
		4	6		1	5		7
	6	5	4	2				1
4				7	9		3	
	5		8	6			1	9
6					4	7	2	5

do you KNOW?

Which flower symbolically means "beauty"?

_____

_____

LETTER LINE

Put a letter in each of the squares below to make a word that means "A JOURNEY." The number clues refer to other words that can be made from the whole.

4 3 10 8 7 SHINE • 5 10 4 8 3 ROYAL

7 8 9 1 2 10 AN INDISCRIMINATE COLLECTOR • 6 7 1 10 5 2 3 ENDANGER

1	2	3	4	5	6	7	8	9	10

High

ACROSS

1 "Mayday!"
5 Mardi Gras necklaces
10 ___ and starts
14 Mishmash
15 Match up
16 Hydroxyl compound
17 World Cup cheers
18 Wander mentally
19 Jean in *The Da Vinci Code*
20 HIGH
22 Revolve around
23 Cecil Day Lewis, e.g.
24 Emmy winner in *Roots*
26 Lets
29 Foremost
32 *Merrie Melodies* stars
33 ___ operandi
34 "Just ___ suspected!"
35 Rob of *Parks and Recreation*
36 Highland fling?
37 "Guys only" party
38 African cobra
39 Took on cargo
40 *Ice Age* sabertooth
41 Swabby
43 Binge
44 Party hearty
45 Flying prefix
46 Kind of role
48 HIGH
53 Hamlet's sister in comics
54 Sky, perhaps
55 Keep from escaping
56 Clive in *Duplicity*
57 Ryan in *Love Story*
58 Relaxation
59 Like valuable stamps
60 Tubular pasta
61 Nerve network

DOWN

1 Mr. Ed's foot
2 She outwrestled Thor
3 Willing, in verse
4 Table
5 Boy Scouts earn them
6 Crane kin
7 Domingo solo
8 Swindled
9 Ready to go
10 José in *The Caine Mutiny*
11 HIGH
12 Rafa Nadal's uncle
13 Where the coin goes
21 "___ that again?"
22 Addition column
25 Instigate
26 African mountains
27 At large
28 HIGH
29 Not plowed
30 Kansas river
31 Strictness
33 Stowe or Albright
36 Be solicitous
37 Nefarious
39 Take a bath
40 Laura in *Rambling Rose*
42 Manx, for one
43 Volkswagen
45 Beelike
46 2011 superhero film
47 Spirit Lake locale
49 Wolverine's group
50 *Dies* ___ (requiem hymn)
51 Huge
52 Olympic sword
54 Cut off

Horoscope

Fill in the grid so that every row, every column, and every frame of six boxes contains six different symbols: health, work, money, happiness, family, and love. Look at the row or column that corresponds with your sign of the zodiac and find out which of the six symbols are important for you today. The symbols appear in increasing order of importance (1–6). It's up to you to translate the meaning of each symbol to your specific situation.

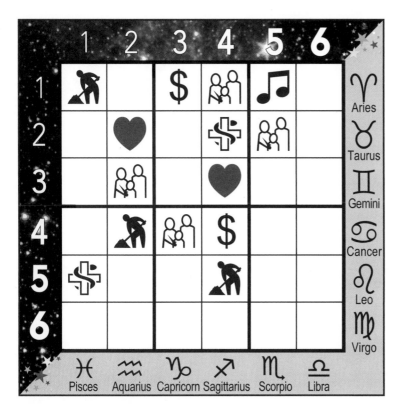

do you KNOW?

Who wrote the bestsellers *Airport* and *Hotel?*

_____

_____

UNCANNY TURN

Rearrange the letters of the phrase below to form a cognate anagram, one that is related or connected in meaning to the original phrase. The answer can be one or more words.

SLID THERE

Kakuro

Each number in a black area is the sum of the numbers that you have to enter in the next empty boxes. The empty boxes that make up the sum are called a run. The sum of the across run is written above the diagonal in the black area, and the sum of the down run is written below the diagonal. Runs can only contain the numbers 1 through 9, and each number in a run can only be used once. The gray boxes only contain odd numbers and the white only even numbers.

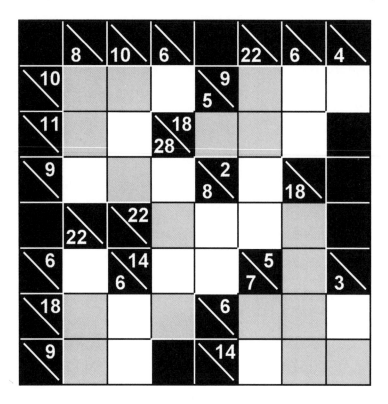

do you KNOW?

How many instruments are there in a string quintet?

70

CROSSWORD Low

ACROSS

1 Bric-a-___
5 Typeface embellishment
10 Most Monets
14 Gray wolf
15 Feminist Jong
16 ___-jerk response
17 Straw in the wind
18 Grand
19 Whoop-de-do
20 LOW
22 One-legged skipper
23 Popeye, to Bluto
24 *The Last Days of Pompeii* heroine
26 Expunge
29 Newfoundland and ___
33 Looseness
34 Bear's disappointment
35 Andalusian article
36 Big top
37 Mountain feature
38 Roman 2,200
39 Suffix for humor
40 Jason's sorceress wife
41 Leaf found in Toronto
42 Taken for granted
44 Stopped, briefly
45 What yardbirds do
46 Make some money
47 Bloke
49 LOW
55 Yale team
56 Apollo's blood
57 Rested
58 Flat fee
59 Become weatherworn
60 Scandinavian royal
61 Lyra's brightest star
62 Taken for a ride
63 Diaphanous

DOWN

1 Special-interest group
2 Plum tomato
3 Harbor a fugitive, e.g.
4 Written agreement
5 Hard to rattle
6 Stiff-backed
7 Major Baltic port
8 Suffix for angel
9 Not perfect
10 Gold medalist Baiul
11 LOW
12 Luke Skywalker's sister
13 Novak Djokovic, for one
21 Roll of the dice
25 "Kid" of jazz
26 Prohibit legally
27 ___-de-lis
28 LOW
29 Loaded cargo
30 Aquarium growth
31 Male relative of Pierre
32 Competed at Indy
34 Midway attraction
37 Corrected
38 World's largest volcano
40 Uncommunicative
41 Anthony in *El Cantante*
43 Nicaraguan snooze
44 Matched up
46 Lyrical verse
47 *Jeopardy* creator Griffin
48 Protected, in boating
50 Tan
51 Place of business
52 South Pacific isle
53 Storyteller
54 Long to change places with

TRIVIA QUIZ   A Brush with Beauty

Test your knowledge about paintings and painters from around
the world with these detailed questions.

1. The French artist Monet is famous for depicting which kind of pond plant?

_____

2. In addition to irises, which flowers are associated with the artist Vincent van Gogh?

_____

3. What American artist was best known for her paintings of enlarged flowers and New Mexico landscapes?

_____

4. Which surrealist often featured strange and twisted clocks in his painting?

_____

5. Which Dutch master painted a picture of the pleasures of the land of Cockaigne?

_____

6. Which medieval Dutch painter is known for nightmarish depictions of the torments of hell?

_____

7. Which painting by Sandro Botticelli depicts a mythical version of the coming of spring?

_____

8. Which great Venetian painter was described as "the sun amidst small stars"?

_____

9. Which American artist was the impetus behind the 1960s Pop Art movement?

_____

10. Which 20th-century Spanish artist was strongly influenced by African art?

_____

11. Where did the French artist Paul Gauguin paint in the 1890s?

_____

12. What American painter was known for his large "drip" style paintings?

_____

13. What name describes paintings of fruit, flowers, food, dead birds, and other inanimate things?

_____

14. What is the name of the painting Johannes Vermeer painted of an imaginary young woman in exotic dress and a large earring?

_____

CROSSWORD 1960s Sitcoms

ACROSS

1 George Ruth's nickname
5 Tout
10 1960 movie *The Parent* _____
14 Candid
15 Dollar bill bird
16 Prefix meaning atmosphere
17 Dress
18 Eva Gabor sitcom (2 wds.)
20 Loathing
22 Family rooms
23 Prefix before verse or corn
24 Name on motor homes
27 Family
28 Rebel Turner
29 TV channel (abbr.)
31 1954-'62 sitcom *Father Knows* _____
33 Less than a min.
35 Cheer
36 Frame
38 Explores the Colorado River
42 Us vs. _____
44 Fencing sword (var.)
46 Request
47 Fries and a salad, e.g.
49 Mrs. Gorbachev
51 Potato relative
52 Part of a file folder
54 1960-'72 sitcom *My Three* _____
55 Eisenhower nickname
56 Sheep sound
59 Vis-à-_____
61 Rule
63 Not on base
64 Earthenware pot
66 Michael, Gabriel or Raphael, e.g.
69 1969-'74 family sitcom *The* _____ (2 wds.)
73 Feed the kitty
74 Indonesian island
75 Golfer Palmer nickname
76 Sushi ingredient
77 Dog's cry
78 Newspaper feature
79 After ginger or cold

DOWN

1 Sale acronym
2 Footless
3 1964-'72 magical sitcom
4 Boredom
5 Implore
6 Paddle
7 Got older
8 Smooth and shiny
9 Venus' sport
10 Tic _____ toe
11 Air a 1960s sitcom
12 Stadium
13 Say something true
19 Lou Grant actor Ed
21 Crowds
25 Disco's the Bee _____
26 "When you wish upon _____" (2 wds.)
29 _____ and crafts
30 Dolphinfish, when repeated
32 Largest brass instruments
34 Fez
37 Before
39 Sally Field sitcom *The* _____ (2 wds.)
40 Patio furniture wood
41 Identical
43 Assembled
45 Serf
48 Type of cabbage
50 Home to 74 Across
53 Spanish city
56 Character on 69 Across
57 Halos
58 "It was nothing _____" (2 wds.)
60 Drink noisily
62 Biting insects
65 _____ *of Green Gables*
67 Sicilian volcano
68 Jump
70 Chip accompaniment
71 Epic hero El _____
72 "_____ So Fine"

Getting Shirty

Which polo shirt (1-5) doesn't belong in this series?

REPOSITION PREPOSITION

Unscramble **NARCOTIC GOD** and find a two-word preposition.

WORD SEARCH Fall Fun

All the words are hidden vertically, horizontally, or diagonally—in both directions.

```
D L L A B T O O F T A G W P I E I L I H C J D R P
Z T C R N G C H R Y S A N T H E M U M N J B W R K
Q E G G P X A E T W O H W B U T C C O S T U M E W
S T U N H G U O D H F S I T R I C K O R T R E A T
P V P R G K B R K P Y W O R C E R A C S G B R X B
J Z A C A P P L E S A U C E L L E A V E S U N I G
V B R A L A B V U E G N I V I G S K N A H T K S K
R N E E W O L L A H F O O Q T I E E I C S P A R Z
Z G J E Z X L O M J W C D D C A F E L M G L J E E
Z G G G T L M E I X K P S Y P E I O O L A L K V R
U E D I R Y A H Z P J P E M S E M L N Z J J P O I
Y E S U O H D E T N U A H T G R K N G O V F O T F
H O P E L N B Z K R G Q I Q G T F A M A C X W F N
O Y S W E A T E R S F V K Q C I D E R J T T S E O
P Q E Z A M N R O C A Y R W F Q C B Z E D E S L B
M L N J S O Q K Z L S N I K P M U P C R I S P N U
T K H B B C N Z S K F B A V Y J G O F G V W U H H
```

- FESTIVALS
- APPLESAUCE
- CHILI
- PIE
- THANKSGIVING
- DOUGHNUTS
- HALLOWEEN
- BONFIRE
- TRICK OR TREAT
- LEFTOVERS
- CHRYSANTHEMUM
- PUMPKINS
- HAYRIDE
- SWEATERS
- COSTUME
- CORN MAZE
- LEAVES
- FOOTBALL
- HAUNTED HOUSE
- CRISP
- CIDER
- RAKE
- TAILGATE
- SCARECROW

Opposites Attract

Match each word with its antonym by writing a number next to each letter.

. . . .

Opposites Attract #1

1. Elated   _____a. Ally

2. Inspired   _____b. Support

3. Lazy   _____c. Beneficial

4. Obscure   _____d. Acknowledge

5. Adversary _____e. Dejected

6. Pernicious _____f. Industrious

7. Oppose   _____g. Ornery

8. Deny   _____h. Ignore

9. Address   _____i. Evident

10. Affable   _____j. Unmotivated

Opposites Attract #2

1. Futile   _____a. Yield

2. Penitent   _____b. Disparaging

3. Boldness   _____c. Unseemly

4. Agreeable _____d. Contrary

5. Defy   _____e. Remorseless

6. Incessant _____f. Loquacious

7. Taciturn   _____g. Useful

8. Careless   _____h. Cowardice

9. Elegant   _____i. Thoughtful

10. Fawning   _____j. Intermittent

TRIVIAL PURSUIT 1976

Americans celebrated 200 years of independence from England with fireworks, parades and other red, white and blue festivities.

MAKE UNCLE SAM PROUD BY SHOWING WHAT YOU RECALL.

1 Who was the U.S. president during the bicentennial?

2 Which president was posthumously promoted to the equivalent of six-star general so he can never be outranked?

3 The bicentennial culminated on July 4 to honor Congress' 1776 adoption of what document?

4 What 6-ton birthday gift did Queen Elizabeth II present to the U.S. on July 6?

5 What denomination of paper currency was issued in 1976?

6 Who unfurled bicentennial and American flags from a 200-foot-high wire at Veterans Stadium in Philadelphia?

7 What singer, dressed in black, served as grand marshal of the American Bicentennial Parade in Washington, D.C.?

8 CBS ran 900 daily short history lessons from 1974 to 1976. What were they called?

TEST YOUR RECALL

Who was the world heavyweight champion in 1976, becoming the first boxer to win three times?

CROSSWORD How Lovely!

ACROSS

1 Petri dish gelatin
5 Blocked from sunlight
10 Ebb antonym
14 Narrative
15 Conical domicile
16 Mote
17 Heron relative
18 "You ___ kidding!"
19 Apt anagram of "vile"
20 Amorous parrot
22 Walking leaf, e.g.
24 Aftershock
25 ___ standstill
26 Groundwork
29 Soda shop order
32 Golfer's dozen
35 Sidewalk marker
37 Pakistani airlines
38 Clarinet's kin
39 Simmons competitor
40 Talk like a toper
41 Escape or Explorer
42 Mrs. Nicolas Sarkozy
43 Fine-grained silt
44 Surround-sound device
46 Pale purple
48 Bats
49 Ducked
53 Auto IDs
56 Romantic goings-on
58 "I swear" may start it
59 Papas or Dunne
61 Golf club feature
62 Fewer than twice
63 The Archfiend
64 Britt of *Desperate Housewives*
65 *The Wizard of Oz* star
66 Cleans up copy
67 Fast bucks?

DOWN

1 Out of whack
2 Eva of *Green Acres*
3 Having a pulse
4 Look like
5 Way up
6 Cologne chap
7 Wasn't original
8 Lounge locale
9 Himalayan hulk
10 Pamplona party
11 Tomato
12 Of the ear
13 Kelly or Disney
21 Pythons
23 DEA agent
27 Cupcake coverer
28 ___ *We Dance* (2004)
29 Emulate Superman
30 Common papal name
31 Teacup handles
32 Head honcho
33 Go right next to
34 No marriage of convenience
36 Jai ___
39 ___ Paulo, Brazil
40 Self-styled
42 End a chess game
43 Wash against
45 Somewhat
47 Carpentry tools
50 Semiconductor device
51 White in *Dreamgirls*
52 Dishearten
53 Shooting match?
54 Lang of Smallville
55 Distaff ___
56 A tribe of Israel
57 "Don't bet ___!"
60 VIP carpet color

BRAINSNACK® Home Port

Which letter is missing in the name of the last port that the yachtsman will enter at the end of his voyage?

NEWPORT
EVERSOR
VOVINO
ORLEMAN
RIMIN?

REPOSITION PREPOSITION

Unscramble **RATTY CROON** and find a two-word preposition.

_____

Mixed Veggies

It won't be hard to get your daily dose of vegetables with these tempting questions.

1. Yosemite Sam is the arch enemy of what carrot-munching cartoon character?

   _____

2. Which explorer is credited with introducing the potato to Europe?

   _____

3. According to the saying, what butters no parsnips?

   _____

4. Which of these is not a vegetable: cabbage, cucumber, cauliflower?

   _____

5. What was Baldrick's favorite vegetable in the TV series *Blackadder*?

   _____

6. Which vegetable is the main ingredient of the Russian soup borscht?

   _____

7. Which bestselling dolls of the 1980s came with their own adoption papers?

   _____

8. Which 1995 animated film brought to life the character of Mr. Potato Head?

   _____

9. Broad, green, and butter are all types of what?

   _____

10. What is the botanical name for a pepper?

    _____

11. What drink, made from a pepper root, is very popular in Fiji?

    _____

12. What is said to be used, along with a stick, to encourage a donkey?

    _____

13. What name is more commonly used for an aubergine?

    _____

14. What foul-smelling fruit from Malaysia is regarded as a delicacy?

    _____

15. What do Americans call the vegetable usually known in Britain as a courgette?

    _____

16. What vegetable gets its name from Old French Latin for milk?

    _____

Sudoku

Fill in the grid so that each row, each column, and each 3 x 3 frame contains every number from 1 to 9.

3					6		9	4
4				9		6		
	9		2		5			
			8				3	
9	8		7		4		5	2
	1				9			
			6		2		7	
		7		1				3
8	6		9					5

do you KNOW?

What role earned Madonna her first Golden Globe?

_____

_____

ONE LETTER LESS OR MORE

The word on the right side contains the letters of the word on the left side, plus or minus the letter in the middle. One letter is already in the right place.

KINGFISH -K ☐ ☐ S ☐ ☐ ☐ ☐

Keep Going

Start on a blank square of your choice and connect as many blank squares as possible with one single continuous line. You can only connect squares along vertical and horizontal lines, not along diagonal lines. You must continue the connecting line up until the next obstacle, i.e., the border of the box, a black square, or a square that has already been used. You can change direction at any obstacle you meet. Each square can only be used once. The number of blank squares that will be left unused is marked in the upper square. There is more than one solution. We only show one solution.

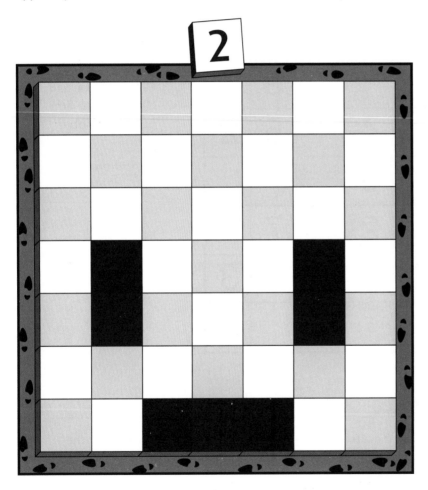

change **ONE**

Change one letter in each of these two words to form a common two-word phrase.
GULL GOWN

82

CROSSWORD # 1970s No. 1 Hits

ACROSS

1 Jason's ship
5 Fantasize
10 Ski lift
14 Chucklehead
15 Utah mountains
16 Folk singer Guthrie
17 1970 hit by the Carpenters
19 Unassisted
20 Miss from Cadiz
21 Dork
23 Falsities
24 Black Forest spa
25 They're out of this world
28 Gargantuan
31 Judo sashes
32 Boxcar hoppers
33 Charlottesville col.
34 Play the wolf
35 Deadly African snake
36 Like fine Scotch
37 Light pat
38 Mudville slugger
39 Frighten
40 Ingredients
42 Red suit
43 Lingerie item
44 Half-moon tide
45 "Das Klagende Lied" composer
47 Lisbon locale
51 "... ___ saw Elba"
52 1971 Carole King hit
54 Arctic seabird
55 Major French river
56 Blondie drummer Burke
57 Sailing
58 Takes second
59 Olive genus

DOWN

1 Basics
2 Othello, e.g.
3 Bullyboy
4 Archaic
5 Import taxes
6 Runs rampant
7 "The Memory of Trees" singer
8 From ___ Z
9 Hawaiian volcano
10 Has a spoonful
11 1971 Rolling Stones hit
12 "___ want for Christmas ..."
13 Carrot, for one
18 Moran and Gray
22 Nuptial exchanges
24 Riggs of tennis
25 Living quarters
26 Type of holiday
27 1970 Jackson 5 hit
28 Hails (from)
29 Forestall
30 Does dock work
32 Like Harvard's pudding
35 Big baboon
36 Cliff-diving Mexican resort
38 Surrender formally
39 NATO's former kin
41 Mercouri in *Never On Sunday*
42 Chivalrous ones
44 U. of ___ Dame
45 "I ___ man with seven ..."
46 Bellicose god
47 23rd Greek letters
48 Chutzpah
49 To ___ (exactly)
50 "Champagne Tony" of golf
53 As well

Futoshiki

Fill in the 5 x 5 grid with the numbers from 1 to 5 once per row and column, while following the greater-than/lesser-than symbols shown. There is only one valid solution that can be reached through logic and clear thinking alone!

			3	
	>		<	
	<	3	>	
				>

CONNECT TWO

An oxymoron is a combination of seemingly contradictory or incongruous words, such as "science fiction" (science means "knowledge or study dealing with facts or truth," while fiction means "an imagined or invented creation"). Connect the words with meanings that oppose each other and make oxymorons.

CALCULATED	SOUND
COUNTLESS	BABY
MUTE	RISK
BIG	NUMBERS

Word Sudoku

Complete the grid so that each row, each column, and each 3 x 3 frame contains the nine letters from the black box below. The hidden nine-letter word is in the diagonal from top left to bottom right.

A D E I L M R T W

				R				
	L		E			A	D	
		T		A				I
		W			R			A
				T				
I					R			
R						T	I	
D			W				E	M
W				M	D			

do you KNOW?

What is Abyssinia now called?

_____

_____

LETTERBLOCKS

Move the letterblocks around so that words associated with business are formed on the top and bottom rows.

Twin Openers 1

ACROSS
1 Burger side
5 Binary star in Perseus
10 Read optically
14 Bose system
15 Dutch cheese
16 Toontown murder victim
17 Turkey's neighbor
18 Like Gandhi
19 Husband of Osiris
20 Termite eater
22 Leaves on the table?
24 Enlightened
25 Chocolate sub
26 Self-proclaimed genius
29 TV adjustment
32 Conductor Previn
33 One of the Corleones
34 Common article
35 ___ to Perdition (2002)
36 Oceanic ray
37 Burn on the outside
38 Sleet-covered
39 Sharply felt
40 Mattress features
41 Chinese metropolis
43 Setting
44 Scale deductions
45 Sow's squeal
46 Goods cast overboard
48 It sticks to your ribs?
52 Salt Lake City locale
53 "Farewell, Pierre!"
55 2010 Disney sci-fi film
56 Carp kin
57 Tibia neighbors
58 Edvard Munch Museum site
59 Forest ruminants
60 Further
61 Dobbin's dinner

DOWN
1 LaBeouf of Transformers
2 Turkish currency
3 Long way off
4 Not on the lee side
5 Dumbstruck
6 Nantes river
7 Icky stuff
8 Idiosyncratic
9 Lake Geneva city
10 Shanty singer
11 2011 Yankee pitcher
12 Betwixt
13 Monstrous Scottish loch
21 Ivy feature
23 Affectedly aesthetic
25 Imaginative tale
26 Stade Roland Garros site
27 Arden of fiction
28 Historic 1944 event
29 Raccoonlike animal
30 Verb of the future
31 Succinct
33 Large seabirds
36 Diagrams
37 Parakeet's cousin
39 Pearl Mosque site
40 Negative aspects
42 Ramblers of yore
43 Part of LCD
45 Like Henry VIII
46 Law in The Aviator
47 List abbr.
48 Kookaburra, e.g.
49 ___ Minor
50 Filly's brother
51 Eve's grandson
54 Will Smith, to Willow

WORD SEARCH · Alpinism

All the words are hidden vertically, horizontally, or diagonally—in both directions. The letters that remain unused form a sentence from left to right.

```
B U I K B R I D G I N G L D S
E R C I S N O P M A R C N G C
B O W L I N E K N O T U S U O
R U D A L L Y K I L C P L L R
E T N G A L O B E H L T I M E
C D A L I O A B I E N M A R B
I O M N H L T M G E G G G O G
G O M T A S N L M F N T H E E
A R O N I E O P X E I T E R H
L O C A Y O I I S O R R O F C
F E W S P U B I U I E L H D T
I N G S Q Q U I C K D R A W I
R O P E I M S L A N L E R W H
K M O U N T A I N S U E N S E
A N C H O R B E N D O X E C V
R O O D N I I S T I B X S N O
R E T T O P S B G H E Y S P L
W E R C S C R A S H P A D E C
```

- ABSEIL
- ANCHOR BEND
- BALANCE
- BOULDERING
- BOWLINE KNOT
- BRIDGING
- CHIMNEYS
- CLOVE HITCH
- COMMAND
- CRAMPONS
- CRASH PAD
- EQUIPMENT
- FLAG
- FOOT HOOK
- GRIP
- HARNESS
- HEXES
- INDOOR
- KNOTS
- LEG LOOP
- MAGNESIUM
- MOUNTAINS
- OUTDOOR
- QUICKDRAW
- ROCK
- ROPE
- SCORE
- SCREW
- SPOTTER
- WAIST BELT

Sudoku Twin

Fill in the grid so that each row, each column, and each 3 x 3 frame contains every number from 1 to 9. A sudoku twin is two connected 9 x 9 sudokus.

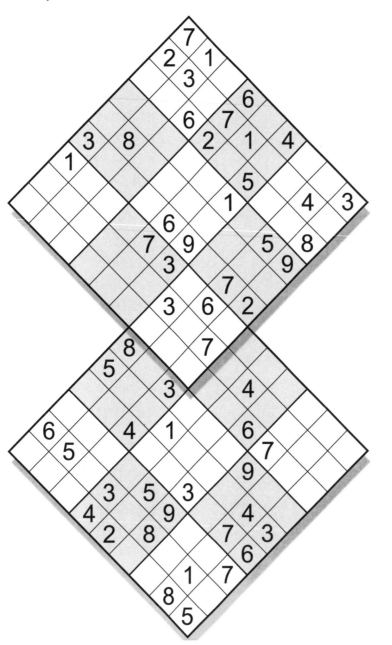

doubletalk

Homophones are words that share the same pronunciation, no matter how they are spelled. If they are spelled differently, then they are called heterographs.

Find heterographs meaning:

A SEAT FOR A KING and **TOSSED**

_____

_____

Sport Maze

Draw the shortest way from the ball to the goal. You can only move along vertical and horizontal lines, not along diagonal lines. The figure on each square indicates the number of squares the ball must be moved in the same direction. You can change direction at each stop.

	2	3	3	5	4
4	2	1	4	1	3
5	1	3	1	2	5
5	2	1	2	3	4
5	2	2	2	4	1
1	4	1	3	2	2

do you KNOW?

Which country won the FIFA World Cup in 1978?

_____

_____

UNCANNY TURN

Rearrange the letters of the phrase below to form a cognate anagram, one that is related or connected in meaning to the original phrase. The answer can be one or more words.

UP CLOSE

Name That Dessert

The chef wants a new name for his dessert, so he writes down a few logical variants. What will the last variant be?

TRANSADDITION

Add one letter to **HI RATTLE AND ROAR** and rearrange the rest to find a connection.

CROSSWORD # At the Lake

ACROSS

1. Fishing need at the lake
5. Little green veggie
8. Amazement
11. Buenos ___, Argentina
13. Rainbow shape
14. Indent
15. Bright reflection
16. Small lakeside home
18. Turkey, pork and beef
20. ___ Rabbit (Uncle Remus character)
21. Fun activity while boating
24. Narrowest part of the torso
25. Leave out
26. Unthinking repetition
29. Pester
30. Past presidential candidate Ross
31. Kitten's foot
34. Singer McEntire
35. Largest brass instrument
36. TV host King
40. Skipping ___ on a still lake
42. Indicated by a lightbulb in cartoons
43. Detroit is the ___ City
45. Large boat for cruising the lake
47. Put pen to paper
51. Anger
52. Buddy
53. Walk sideways
54. Condensation that forms overnight
55. One or more
56. Pier

DOWN

1. Witch
2. Canola ___
3. Are you a man ___ mouse? (2 words)
4. Famous green puppet
5. Covenant, deal
6. Greek god of love
7. Part of a play
8. Old name in video games
9. Paychecks
10. Film critic Roger
12. Witnessed
17. Abbreviation on a schedule
19. Come to the same conclusion
21. Heavy weight
22. Actress Thurman
23. Large
24. Covered with moisture
27. Sphere
28. Breakfast choice
30. Be nosy
31. Play on words
32. Lincoln nickname
33. Used to be
35. Sizzling
36. Substance insoluble in water
37. Love
38. Restore
39. City rodent
41. Hauls
43. Whimper
44. Just
46. Greek exclamation
48. Vow words
49. Solicitous consideration (abbrev.)
50. Word of fright

Honeycomb Crossword

Not all crosswords are square. On this page, you are invited to fit the words into an altogether more complex geometry.

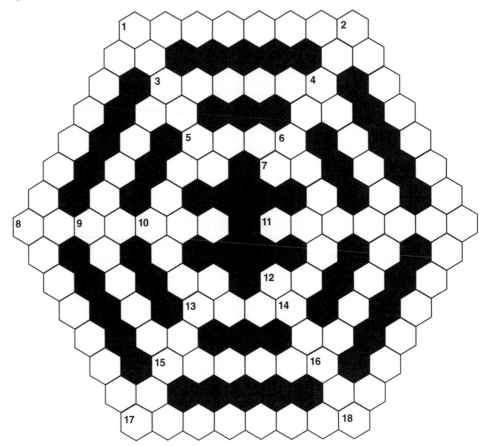

TRAVEL EAST

1 Reverie (8)
3 Cell specialized to transmit impulses in the body (6)
5 Form of silicate mineral used in industry for insulation (4)
8 Fine, stiff dress material (7)
11 Small, dried seedless grape (7)
13 To make designs on metal or glass using acid to eat out the lines (4)
15 Confection containing chopped nuts and cherries (6)
17 Frantic migration to prospect the Klondike, for example, in the 1890s (8)

TRAVEL NORTH-EAST

7 Champagne or wine bottle holding 1.5 liters (6)
8 A Feudal ruler (8)
9 The raised arm on a sundial (6)
10 A standard or typical way of behaving (4)
14 German equivalent of Mister (4)
16 Treeless regions of the Northern Hemisphere lying just south of the polar ice cap (6)

17 River that flows into the Bay of Bengal and is sacred to the Indian people (6)
18 One whose lifestyle is devoted to the seeking of pleasure (8)

TRAVEL SOUTH-EAST

1 An electric generator (6)
2 First name of the author of Gone With the Wind (8)
4 American state, capital Carson City (6)
6 Tree, also known as Maple (4)

8 Extroverted and friendly (8)
9 Unit of capacity equal to 8 pints (6)
10 Number of planets in our Solar System (4)
12 Roof covering of straw or reeds (6)

BRAIN FITNESS # Star-Crossed

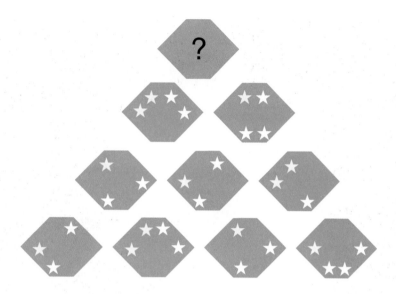

Which option below should replace the question mark at the top of the pyramid?

A   B   C   D   E

Masquerade

Which color (1–10) should replace the question mark?

DOODLE PUZZLE

A doodle puzzle is a combination of images, letters, and/or numbers that represent a word or a concept. If you cannot solve a doodle puzzle, do not look at the answer right away. Think hard—and outside the box.

CROSSWORD # Twin Openers 2

ACROSS

1 Code word for "A"
5 Location
10 Puts in stitches
14 Antony or Chagall
15 Bar twist
16 Pressure from the cops
17 Nonesuch
18 ___-garde
19 Light brown shade
20 Founding member of Judas Priest
22 Mouse's find
23 Apiphobe's fear
24 Violinist Zimbalist
26 On ship
29 Indy racer Luyendyk
30 AWOL arresters
33 Cite verbatim
34 Sherlock's love
35 Gershwin or Newborn
36 Heidi's home
37 Did some karate
38 Cross condition
39 Air-gun ammo
40 Of birth
41 Greek S
42 Remote battery
43 Foamy drinks
44 Dark blue plum
45 Whirlpool appliance
47 Highway exit
48 Santa ___
50 *How Green Was My Valley* novelist
55 Exodus plague
56 *Fantastic Mr. Fox* author Dahl
57 Lionel Richie song
58 Alternative word
59 Month for fools
60 "Peter Pan" pirate
61 Tampa Bay team
62 "___ Train": Cat Stevens
63 Certain raspberry pastry

DOWN

1 Frenzied
2 Gangly
3 Allen of radio days
4 Circus stars
5 Smoothed wood
6 Jeans
7 "Walk Like ___": The Four Seasons
8 Snaky fish
9 Tolkien's Treebeard
10 Khan in *The Jungle Book*
11 *Tulips & Chimneys* author
12 Toasty
13 Paycheck leftover
21 "You ___ Meant for Me"
22 Ontario native
25 Pinpoint
26 Jordan seaport
27 *Taras ___*: Gogol
28 "Clumsy me!"
29 Zones
31 First-class
32 The Archfiend
34 Butt in
37 Curly-leaf cabbage
38 Most elementary
40 Opposing votes
41 Equivalent
44 Loiter
46 Parameters
47 Museum piece
48 Loire tributary
49 "Deck the Halls" syllables
51 Yuri Zhivago's love
52 Tibetan monk
53 Flanders river
54 Russian negative
56 Grammy category

Television in 1948 began to change the way we spent our evenings. Americans were eager to buy the luxuries (cars, houses, and televisions) denied to them during WWII. And all four networks—ABC, CBS, NBC and DuMont (now defunct)— began to broadcast shows during prime time.

WHICH OF THESE EARLY OFFERINGS DO YOU STILL REMEMBER?

1 Milton Berle, TV's first superstar, starred in this early vaudeville-style variety series.

2 Adults and children alike adored this live ad-libbed puppet show on NBC.

3 Ted Mack hosted this precursor to *The Gong Show* and *American Idol*.

4 Ed Sullivan showcased top talent on this long-running variety series. Its original name?

5 NBC still airs this public affairs show that puts powerful people on the spot.

6 Allen Funt pranked unsuspecting people for laughs on this early reality show.

7 Hollywood's future stars appeared live in this dramatic anthology series.

8 What hours are considered prime time in Central/Mountain time?

TEST YOUR RECALL

Who was the 45th Vice President of the United States, born in March 1948?

CROSSWORD # Chairman of the Board

ACROSS

1 Twosome
5 Pole of Highland games
10 Foundling
14 Fairytale opener
15 Light of foot
16 Not pro
17 1958 Frank Sinatra hit
19 "___ a Kick Out of You"
20 Strives to match
21 Comes out with
23 Remnant
24 Oliver's porridge
25 Votes against
26 Not abstract
29 Less than always
32 She played the 10 in *10*
33 Desire
34 Cowardly Lion portrayer
35 Cryptic
36 Ward off
37 Eggs
38 Atkinson in *Mr. Bean*
39 Doesn't die out
40 Storekeeper, e.g.
42 Palindromic parent
43 Boxer's seat
44 "Everybody ___ Cha Cha Cha": Cooke
48 They earned their wings
50 Nelly Furtado song
51 *Alias* Emmy winner Lena
52 1966 Frank Sinatra hit
54 Under lock and key
55 MacDowell in *Beauty Shop*
56 Feed the kitty
57 Starry-___ idealist
58 *Star Wars: Episode I* director
59 Bela's *Son of Frankenstein* role

DOWN

1 Strength
2 Japanimation
3 Metrical accent
4 Easy chair
5 Prickly pear
6 Jibe
7 Hate crime cause
8 Brownie
9 Went back
10 One to tip
11 1958 Frank Sinatra hit
12 Anatomical duct
13 Is the right size
18 Modeled
22 Sherwood Forest friar
24 Bridge maven
26 Closet wood
27 Pavilion
28 Puts a halt to
29 Swan genus
30 Pet, slangily
31 1966 Frank Sinatra hit
32 Carpenter's peg
35 Gargantuan
36 Fallback jump shot
38 Real cutup
39 Melbourne's Rod ___ Arena
41 Expiated
42 Presentees
44 Female vampire
45 "Fields of Gold" singer
46 Fifty minutes past
47 Directive
48 It's sometimes struck
49 "Now ___ me down ..."
50 2600, to Caesar
53 Burma's first prime minister

Literature

All the words are hidden vertically, horizontally, or diagonally—in both directions. The letters that remain unused form a sentence from left to right.

```
P  L  I  T  E  R  A  E  L  R  Y  A  U  T  H
O  O  P  L  O  T  P  L  E  G  E  N  D  R  S
E  W  A  N  T  I  T  Y  V  Y  A  S  S  E  B
M  O  P  C  C  N  O  R  O  M  Y  X  O  A  O
P  F  C  A  N  O  N  I  N  O  V  E  L  L  A
N  O  I  V  R  E  Y  C  L  A  M  L  E  S  S
D  U  E  C  A  O  L  A  A  Y  A  G  E  W  T
W  I  A  T  T  I  D  L  N  D  I  T  H  N  R
F  E  A  E  B  I  T  Y  O  E  H  E  E  I  A
A  S  I  R  D  R  O  T  I  M  M  M  E  X  V
I  T  A  V  Y  N  T  N  G  O  H  Y  M  N  E
R  R  L  S  E  I  O  N  E  C  A  N  T  A  L
Y  U  L  M  R  R  O  R  R  O  H  T  I  H  S
T  C  E  O  M  E  T  A  P  H  O  R  S  T  T
A  T  G  T  I  C  P  T  E  K  C  O  P  P  O
L  U  O  I  M  C  R  I  T  I  Q  U  E  L  R
E  R  R  F  A  N  E  T  O  D  C  E  N  A  Y
N  E  Y  S  C  I  T  A  M  A  R  D  E  Y  R
```

- ALLEGORY
- ANECDOTE
- BALLAD
- CANON
- COMEDY
- CRITIQUE
- DIARY
- DRAMATICS
- EPIC
- ESSAY
- FAIRY TALE
- FICTION
- HORROR
- HYMN
- LEGEND
- LIBRARY
- LYRICAL
- METAPHOR
- MOTIF
- MYTH
- NOVELLA
- OXYMORON
- PARCHMENT
- PARODY
- PLAY
- PLOT
- POCKET
- POEM
- POET
- REGIONAL NOVEL
- REVIEW
- RONDEAU
- STRUCTURE
- TRAVEL STORY

Sudoku

Fill in the grid so that each row, each column, and each 3 x 3 frame contains every number from 1 to 9.

4	7	9		1				2
3	5	6						
2							9	3
	9		2		1		4	
1		8	3	7	9		5	6
	7				4			9
8			1			6		5
						3		7
				8				

do you KNOW?

What is Mimolette?

_____

_____

ONE LETTER LESS OR MORE

The word on the right side contains the letters of the word on the left side, plus or minus the letter in the middle. One letter is already in the right place.

B A C K D O O R +L [ ] [ ] A [ ] [ ] [ ] [ ] [ ]

Famous Leos

ACROSS

1 Sellouts
5 Twig broom
10 Upscale cameras
14 Pronto, initially
15 Bogart's *High Sierra* role
16 Drudgery
17 Leo actor
20 *The Stepford Wives* protagonist
21 Tested, as a load
22 Biol. and geol.: Abbr.
24 Golden Calf deity
25 African adventure series (1966–69)
28 Tempers
32 Olympic swords
33 "Big ___" (David Ortiz)
35 Month before *juin*
36 Leo film director
40 Wahine's wreath
41 Rice-A-___
42 Soil
43 1935 Masters winner Gene
46 Bose products
48 Pulls a fast one
49 Ankles
50 Criticism
53 African grasslands
57 Leo NBA great
61 In a line
62 Mystery Writers of America award
63 Prefix for bus
64 "Take ___ your leader"
65 Fiend
66 Like Felix Unger

DOWN

1 Muslim pilgrimage
2 Golfer Aoki
3 Blue Nile source
4 Old maid
5 Ritzy part of L.A.
6 Piercing site
7 Mex. lady
8 *No Country for ___ Men* (2007)
9 Wrench user
10 Quash
11 SoHo apartment
12 Abundantly prevalent
13 Flexible Flyer
18 Box eggs
19 Rangy
23 Suction devices
24 Protestant denomination
25 Super buys
26 Cop ___ (beg for leniency)
27 Fermented milk drink
29 Con ___ (lovingly, in music)
30 Milk prefix
31 Turbaned Punjabis
34 Rhone tributary
37 Caught in a cloudburst
38 Ward ___ (local politico)
39 Church music maker
44 Intermission follower
45 Suffix with paleo-
47 Place to order a round
50 Competed in 500 freestyle
51 Spare item
52 Loads
54 Diana Rigg's title
55 Cohen-Chang on *Glee*
56 Uptight state
58 Citrus beverage
59 *Grand Hotel* studio
60 Vietnamese emperor ___ Dai

BRAINSNACK® **Pick A Side**

Which view (1–5) of this castle is wrong?

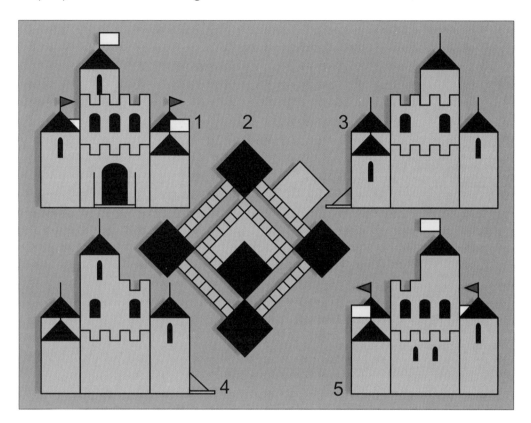

DOODLE PUZZLE

A doodle puzzle is a combination of images, letters, and/or numbers that represent a word or a concept. If you cannot solve a doodle puzzle, do not look at the answer right away. Think hard—and outside the box.

Binairo

Complete the grid with zeros and ones until there are 5 zeros and 6 ones in every row and every column. No more than two of the same number can be next to or under each other. Rows or columns with exactly the same content are not allowed. There is only one valid solution.

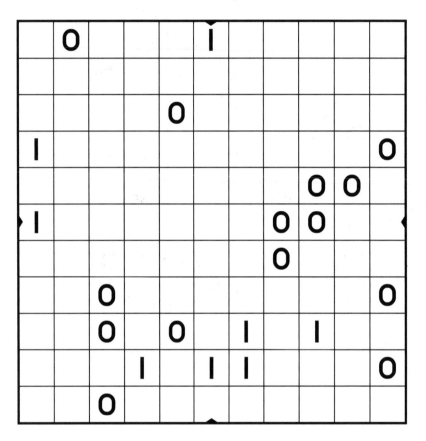

do you KNOW?

What city is home to Botany Bay National Park?

_____

_____

SANDWICH

What five-letter word belongs between the word at left and the word at right, so that the first and second word, and the second and third word, each form a common compound word or phrase?

ELK _ _ _ _ _ DOG

Sport Maze

Draw the shortest way from the ball to the goal. You can only move along vertical and horizontal lines, not along diagonal lines. The figure on each square indicates the number of squares the ball must be moved in the same direction. You can change direction at each stop.

0	3	3	3	1	4
1	4	3	2	1	4
1	2	3	1	2	4
1	2	1	0	1	
1	3	1	4	2	2
3	5	3	1	2	3

do you KNOW?

Where is the anterior cruciate ligament located?

_____

_____

UNCANNY TURN

Rearrange the letters of the phrase below to form a cognate anagram, one that is related or connected in meaning to the original phrase. The answer can be one or more words.

THE COUGARS

Keep Going

Start on a blank square of your choice and connect as many blank squares as possible with one single continuous line. You can only connect squares along vertical and horizontal lines, not along diagonal lines. You must continue the connecting line up until the next obstacle, i.e., the border of the box, a black square, or a square that has already been used. You can change direction at any obstacle you meet. Each square can only be used once. The number of blank squares that will be left unused is marked in the upper square. There is more than one solution. We only show one solution.

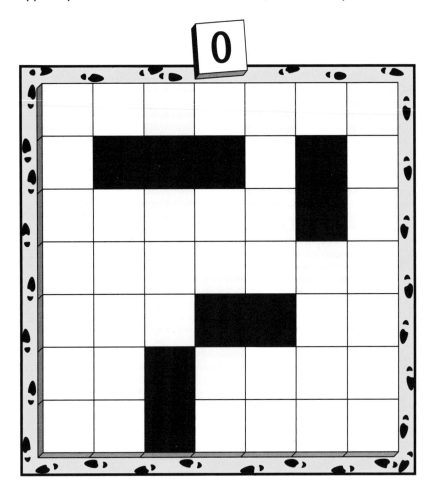

Word Sudoku

Complete the grid so that each row, each column, and each 3 x 3 frame contains the nine letters from the black box below. The hidden nine-letter word is in the diagonal from top left to bottom right.

A	D	G	I	M	R	S	T	U

				S		D		I
U	D	I		T				A
T	I			A				
G		T	U	D	S		R	
			A			T		
U		T	S	I		G	A	
A	U							
M					D	S		
		R						T

do you KNOW

Who designed the Guggenheim Museum in Bilbao?

_____

_____

LETTERBLOCKS

Move the letterblocks around so that words associated with energy are formed on the top and bottom rows.

B	I	A	S	S	O	M
C	O	O	T	S	M	P

Fall Baking

ACROSS

1. Fall baking ingredient
4. ___, vidi, vici
8. Picnic pests
12. *Bird ___ Wire* (2 words)
13. It is often blue or brown
14. Source of feta
15. Hockey great Bobby
16. Fall baking ingredient
18. First appearance
20. Quickly
21. Center
23. Current (with "up," 2 words)
27. Fall baking ingredient
31. Domesticated
32. President Lincoln
33. Civil or Revolutionary
35. ___-Ida potatoes
36. College VIPs
39. Fall baking ingredient
42. Creek
44. Test for an aspiring attorney
45. Regrettably
47. Christmas Eve Santa tracker
51. Fall baking ingredient, ___ squash
55. Compass direction
56. Tennis great Arthur
57. ___ Western Reserve University
58. Hartsfield-Jackson airport code
59. High schooler
60. October birthstone
61. Fall baking dessert

DOWN

1. Devil's ___ cake
2. With regard to (2 words)
3. Clothing
4. Someone who is hurt
5. Blunder
6. Actresses Vardalos and Long
7. All that glitters ___ gold (2 words)
8. Docket
9. Neither fish ___ fowl
10. Road-making material
11. Pig pen
17. Kick out
19. Actress Thurman
22. Grass moisture
24. Run ___ (go haywire)
25. Actress Hatcher
26. Paradise
27. Scoundrels
28. Illegally aid
29. Raise
30. Circuit
34. Massage
37. Clean up
38. Discount
40. Part of a fireplace
41. Expert
43. Explorer Polo
46. Split in two
48. ___ what you sow
49. Against
50. Erase
51. Flying mammal
52. Employ
53. *Hail to ___ Chief*
54. DC is its capital

BRAINSNACK® **Carnival**

Which two letters are missing in the conversation between the two
Venetian carnival merrymakers?

REPOSITION PREPOSITION

Unscramble **FEW RETICENT HERO** and find a three-word preposition.

_____

Outlines

Which letter has the wrong outline color?

DOODLE PUZZLE

A doodle puzzle is a combination of images, letters, and/or numbers that represent a word or a concept. If you cannot solve a doodle puzzle, do not look at the answer right away. Think hard—and outside the box.

CROSSWORD Camping Out

ACROSS
1. Camping trip activity
5. Cellulite
9. Alias (abbrev.)
12. Norse god
13. Flight prefix
14. Groovy
15. Daddy
16. Tell ghost stories around the ___
18. Timid
20. Support for a canvas
21. State ___, popular camping site
24. Peaceful
25. Full grown
26. Metal tube
27. Born
28. Animal doc
29. Sprite
32. Abel's brother
34. Type of brick
36. Pageant, march
39. Camping treat with marshmallows and chocolate
40. Amphitheater
41. Actor Danny of *White Christmas*
42. ___ bag, camping gear
44. Mining waste
48. Actor Danson
49. Oak, for example
50. IX
51. Type of curve
52. Visualizes
53. Protection for campers

DOWN
1. Move like a bunny
2. Ore-___, potato processor
3. Basic move on uneven parallel bars
4. Nail polish
5. One side of a cut gem
6. Drip
7. Tentacle
8. Little ___, shepherdess (2 words)
9. Get up
10. Singer Carpenter
11. "Rolling in the Deep" singer
17. Ticket
19. Florida time, e.g. (abbrev.)
21. Devotee
22. Poetic tribute
23. Regret
24. Take a seat
26. Farm enclosure
28. Compete
29. ___ sale by owner
30. Honest ___
31. Affirmative
32. Walking aid
33. Acclimates
34. Actress Poehler
35. What ___ kill you makes you stronger
36. Glue
37. French city
38. Wetland plants
39. Wise ones
41. Leg joint
43. Anger
45. Fib
46. Columnist Landers
47. Acquire

Word Sudoku

Complete the grid so that each row, each column, and each 3 x 3 frame contains the nine letters from the black box below. The hidden nine-letter word is in the diagonal from top left to bottom right.

D	E	I	L	P	R	S	U	Y

S			L			Y		E
								P
	L	R	I					U
E				L				Y
	D	I		R				
L	S					U		
	I	P						
			D			R		
			Y					

do you KNOW?

"Love apple" is an old name for which fruit?

_____

_____

LETTERBLOCKS

Move the letterblocks around so that words associated with kitchenware are formed on the top and bottom rows. In some blocks, the letter from the top row has been switched with the letter from the bottom row.

I	M	S	P	E	R	M
A	T	S	K	L	A	U

Word Pyramid

Each word in the pyramid has the letters of the word above it, plus a new letter.

E
(1) Exist
(2) Unit of sound intensity equal to 10 decibels
(3) Capable
(4) Piece of furniture
(5) Horse barn
(6) Conflicts
(7) Used in a car or plane to hold you in your seat

do you KNOW?

Who created
the character
Peter Pan?

_____

_____

Sudoku

Fill in the grid so that each row, each column, and each 3 x 3 frame contains every number from 1 to 9.

4	9		8			7	5	
						6		1
	5	6	1	7			9	2
5		9		1			4	7
7				9			6	
1		3		4				
		8			5			
			6					
	4			3		1		

do you KNOW?

Whose aircraft was named *Spirit of St. Louis?*

_____

_____

ONE LETTER LESS OR MORE

The word on the right side contains the letters of the word on the left side, plus or minus the letter in the middle. One letter is already in the right place.

E I N S T E I N +V ☐ ☐ ☐ ☐ N ☐ ☐ ☐ ☐

CROSSWORD Themeless

ACROSS
1 The ___ of March (2011)
5 Buddhist shrine
10 Annoys
14 Boston cager, for short
15 Vietnamese capital
16 Fender flaw
17 Budgie is a little one
19 Brainchild
20 Handel opus
21 Befitting
23 White knight
24 Candied, in cookery
25 48 ___ (Nick Nolte film)
26 Tasmanian duckbill
29 Diamond feature
32 Bearings
33 Palm smartphone
34 "Just my luck!"
35 Pasta pick
36 Dispatched
37 "Hi-De-Ho Man" Calloway
38 Frankenstein, for one
39 Too severe
40 Broadcast
42 Prohibit
43 Did an axel
44 Focus of LAX screenings
48 Make waves
50 Plundered
51 Meter man?
52 "Blue" singer
54 Bugbear
55 Say "li'l," say
56 What a stitch in time saves
57 Yosemite Sam, for one
58 Yellow weed
59 And others

DOWN
1 Blood of the gods
2 "John ___ Tractor": Judds
3 Greek name for Greece
4 Baseball features
5 Coasts
6 Malayan mammal
7 "Golden Rule" word
8 "Annabel Lee" poet
9 Boeing product
10 Dumbness
11 Cayenne flakes
12 ___-jerk reaction
13 Hexagram
18 Place for a net
22 Charlie Brown's cry
24 Close in Albert Nobbs
26 Burgundy grape
27 Footed vases
28 Clockmaker Thomas
29 Truism
30 Winglike
31 Southwestern horseman
32 Be worthy of
35 Booklet
36 Cheerfully optimistic
38 Ag degrees
39 Viking of comics
41 Spruce up
42 Fife or Frank
44 Rings
45 Come clean about
46 Davis in Tootsie
47 Ford of dubious fame
48 Catch sight of
49 Cartoon possum
50 Open ocean
53 She, in Lisbon

Big Words 1

ACROSS

1 Homes to squirrels
5 Passover feast
10 Click-on image
14 Football foul
15 Make amends
16 Spanish cat
17 Pitchfork prong
18 "Is ___ dagger which I see ...": Shak.
19 Noncoms
20 Foolish
22 Very particular
24 Differentiate
25 Metric volume measure
26 Long-handled tool
27 Short dagger
30 Aura, slangily
33 Work on the cutting edge?
34 Groovy
35 *The Dukes of Hazzard* deputy
36 Catalonia locale
37 Artist Rockwell
38 Suffix for Catholic
39 *Enterprise* officer
40 Contents of Santa's mail
41 Maine crustaceans
43 Go down swinging
44 Incompetent
45 Jeff in *True Grit*
49 Send into exile
51 Gossip
52 Collect in return
53 Shake a tail
55 Joy Adamson's cat
56 Puccini's "Vissi d'___"
57 Time in power
58 Persian Gulf missile
59 Food colorings
60 Napped
61 "___ Leaving Home": Beatles

DOWN

1 Double quartet
2 Suspect's story
3 Types
4 Soliloquies
5 Burlesque
6 Frome of fiction
7 Kill
8 Funny pair?
9 Response
10 Turn a deaf ear to
11 Mania
12 Great Plains Indians
13 Like a yenta
21 Speed Wagons
23 Beatles album
25 Small groove
27 Has the leading role
28 Smoke glass
29 ___ out (withdraws)
30 One of seven for Salome
31 ___ many words
32 Make a buzzing noise
33 Burst of energy
36 Police dog
37 Benignity
39 All-purpose trucks
40 Put down carpet
42 Wesley in *U.S. Marshals*
43 Good buddy
45 Stir slightly
46 Flash flood area
47 Follow as a consequence
48 Heaps
49 Pitt in *Moneyball*
50 Wispy
51 Pop test
54 Burnett of advertising

BRAINSNACK® Missing Corner

Which cube (1–6) fits in the empty corner?

TRANSADDITION

Add one letter to **HUNT STAR FRINGES** and rearrange the rest to find a connection.

_____

Sunny

Where will the sun shine? With the knowledge that each arrow points to a place where a symbol should be, can you locate the sunny spots? The symbols cannot be next to each other, vertically, horizontally, or diagonally. A symbol cannot be placed on top of an arrow. We show one symbol.

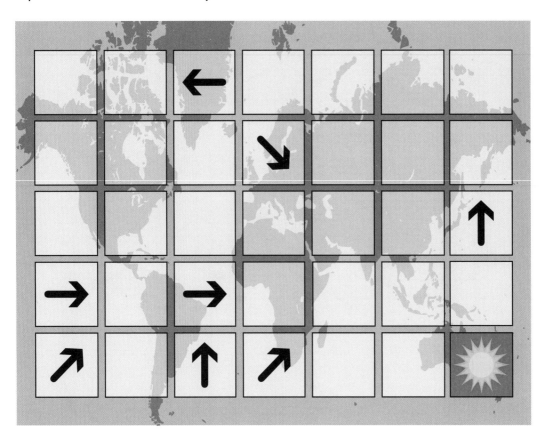

BLOCK ANAGRAM

Form the word that is described in the parentheses using the letters above the grid. An extra letter ais already in the right place.

BANKERS (U.S. State)

						A

CROSSWORD Eastwood Films

ACROSS

1 Filter through
5 Out of place
10 Hebrew month
14 West End opener
15 Extend a note
16 River near the Red Sea
17 "I confess that I have no desire to confess." film
19 Fumble
20 Defers
21 Austrian cakes
23 Canadian loonies
24 Cyrus of *Hannah Montana*
25 Increasingly sore
28 To an extent
31 Research funds
32 Squad car sound
33 Rosary bead
34 Isn't misused?
35 Joined forces
36 Hebrides hill
37 *Family Guy* daughter
38 Susann's *Valley of the ___*
39 Yellow finch
40 Good enough
42 How acrobats perform
43 Childhood illness
44 "Love Song" singer Bareilles
45 Mumbai masters
47 Mood
51 Viking war god
52 "I seen the angel of death, he's got snake eyes." film
54 Boxers and pugs
55 Sorghum
56 Call for
57 Silvery
58 Trample
59 Spaces between teeth

DOWN

1 Drops off
2 Beige
3 Greek vowels
4 Zero in on
5 Laundry employee
6 Dweebs
7 Black cuckoos
8 Pigsty
9 Double-crossed
10 Prince Harry's uncle
11 "I know what you're thinking, punk." film
12 Hydrocortisone additive
13 Sales folks
18 Palindromic principle
22 *Victory Square* novelist Steinhauer
24 Societal customs
25 Long-tailed lizard
26 Shed tears
27 "You don't remember me, do you?" film
28 Crabwalk
29 Be of help
30 Extremely small
32 River deposits
35 Lather
36 Scolding
38 Not too bright
39 Watercress piece
41 Tonsil disorder
42 Despot
44 Squall
45 Cutty Sark cutter
46 Commotions
47 Do of the '60s
48 Eye membrane
49 Not superficial
50 Tim Tebow targets
53 Head case

Number Cluster

Cubes showing numbers have been placed on the grid below, with some spaces left empty. Can you complete the grid by creating runs of the same number and of the same length as the number? So, where a cube with number 5 has been included on the grid, you need to create a run of five number 5's, including the cube already shown. The run can be horizontal, vertical, or both horizontal and vertical.

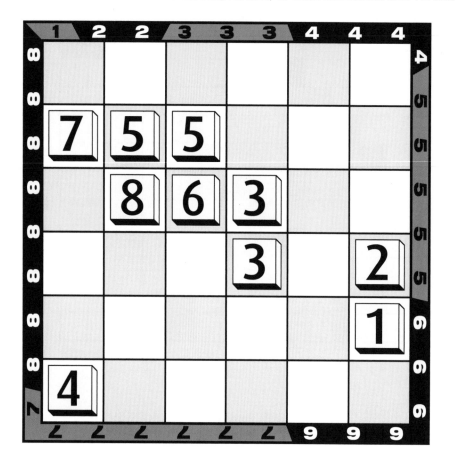

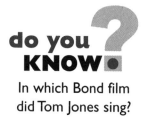

do you KNOW?

In which Bond film did Tom Jones sing?

_____

_____

Spot the Differences

Find the nine differences in the image on the bottom right.

do you KNOW?

Who attended the Mad Hatter's tea party?

_____

_____

trivia

• What language do the Amish speak?

_____

Vegan Special

ACROSS

1 Big Band music
6 Informal eatery
10 Mudpuppies
14 Norse pantheon
15 Libra birthstone
16 Bound to happen
17 Dense fogs
19 "Remembrance of a Garden" artist
20 Sugar suffix
21 One of the Munsters
23 Dinette set spot
27 Jimmy Eat World's music
28 Pride Lands female
30 Beatles song from *Let It Be*
34 Crimson-clad
35 *A Lesson From* ___: Fugard
37 Victoria's Secret purchase
38 Rowlands in *Hope Floats*
39 Fred and George Weasley, e.g.
40 Kind of ticket
41 "So there!"
42 Sleazy
43 Tropical vine
44 Reliable
46 Breastbone
48 Reggae precursor
49 1992 Wimbledon winner
50 Daytona Beach wear
54 Prefix for pod
55 Poland border river
56 *Toy Story* toy (with "Mr.")
62 Saucy
63 Spanker, for one
64 Present purpose
65 Drive by
66 Mideast cartel
67 Romance author Danielle

DOWN

1 Aphid's lunch
2 Petite
3 "Love ___ Simple Thing"
4 Grafton's ___ *for Noose*
5 Like LPs
6 Deal with
7 Simian
8 Work the land
9 Mexican model Benitez
10 Baffin Island native
11 Badly mistaken
12 It beats the deuce
13 Observed
18 Applications
22 Vintage vehicles
23 Ablaze
24 One-dimensional
25 U. of Nebraska team
26 Eligible for service
29 Worked in a lumber mill
30 *The Book of Mormon* awards
31 Basketball great Unseld
32 Oberon's planet
33 Cold-cuts choice
36 Hard cover
39 Undershirt
40 Sorvino in *Sweet Nothing*
42 *South Park* character
43 Scores
45 Mini and maxi
47 Sharp
50 Comet Hale-___
51 Conceit
52 ___ facto
53 Hotel freebie
54 Bathroom sprinkle
57 Musical link
58 Hard to keep in stock
59 Yale-to-Harvard direction
60 Pass with flying colors
61 Juan ___ Potro of tennis

Sport Maze

Draw the shortest way from the ball to the goal. You can only move along vertical and horizontal lines, not along diagonal lines. The figure on each square indicates the number of squares the ball must be moved in the same direction. You can change direction at each stop.

3	5	5	5	1	2
2	3	1	2	3	4
3	2	1	3	3	2
5	4	2	3	3	5
2	1	4	1	2	
2	2	1	5	1	2

do you KNOW

Who is younger, Serena or Venus Williams?

_____

_____

UNCANNY TURN

Rearrange the letters of the phrase below to form a cognate anagram, one that is related or connected in meaning to the original phrase.

NO STAMP

Environment

All the words are hidden vertically, horizontally, or diagonally—in both directions. The letters that remain unused form a sentence from left to right.

```
C O N S E R V A T I O N D E E
E R U T L U C I R G A G E C R
R A I N F O R E S T O V R O O
D A N G E R O U S A E R E L S
N S O L A R P A N E L N G O I
O T O Y K M E I N T S A N G O
I R N D S O M M C I A L A Y N
S O A N U A F H A O R G D A N
E P I Z L Y G R E N E D N I W
P E A S T T I O N A U S E A T
O R T E I M P T T O L R P R O
L T E D T C N I T X E T E C T
L T E H N O I T A R D Y H E D
U S U S T A I N A B L E E A E
T N F U N C T I O N A L V R I
I L I G H T P O L L U T I O N
O R O N G N I L C Y C E R L M
N E N O Z O N E L A Y E R F T
```

- AGRICULTURE
- ANIMALS
- CONSERVATION
- DANGEROUS
- DEHYDRATION
- ECOLOGY
- ENDANGERED
- EROSION
- EXTINCT
- FAUNA
- FLORA
- FUNCTIONAL
- HEALTH
- KYOTO
- LIGHT POLLUTION
- MANURE
- NOISE POLLUTION
- OZONE LAYER
- RAIN FOREST
- RECYCLING
- REPORT
- SOLAR PANEL
- SUSTAINABLE
- TIDES
- WIND ENERGY

CROSSWORD **Famous Sagittarians**

ACROSS

1 Ibuprofen target
5 Cleveland's Gund
10 Bones of *Sleepy Hollow*
14 Made some beds
15 German engraver
16 Eisenhower, to MacArthur
17 Sagittarian actor
20 Handbook
21 Willows for weavers
22 November 11 honoree
24 Son of Ares
25 Georgia's capital
29 Morty and Ferdie, to Mickey
33 Engine conduit
34 Peninsula near Hong Kong
36 Third of XXI
37 Sagittarian novelist
41 Undershirt
42 Sniffers
43 Sacramento arena
44 Bride of Dionysus
46 Fertilized eggs
49 Burns out
50 Up for payment
51 Signs of indifference
54 Chinese meditative exercises
59 Sagittarian painter
63 Death notice
64 Flout the rules
65 Beak part
66 Lily who sang soprano
67 As a result
68 Take notice

DOWN

1 "Excuse me ..."
2 Ballet conclusion
3 Chopped down
4 Jacob's hairy brother
5 Confuses
6 Scatter ___
7 Walk in a run
8 Classic beginning
9 Tree-dwelling
10 Expel
11 Bailiff's command
12 Sulfur attribute
13 Clothing store section
18 Norah Jones' father
19 14-legged crustacean
23 L.A. and London dailies
24 Like Tiffany displays
25 Eighth Greek letter
26 Hole-making bug
27 Japanese immigrant
28 Albanian coin
30 "___ inch a king!": Shak.
31 Word after "roger"
32 Grain holders
35 Big name in bandages
38 Deep blue
39 Peerless
40 No-brainer card game
45 18-and-over crowd
47 Change in form
48 Bridges in *Norma Rae*
51 "Freeze!"
52 Emmett Kelly role
53 Once-great city, perhaps
55 Chickenpox symptom
56 Canadian tribe
57 Companion of now
58 Secured
60 Pronoun for a plane
61 Dark time, to a bard
62 Varnish substance

Sudoku X

Fill in the grid so that each row, each column, and each 3 x 3 frame contains every number from 1 to 9. The two main diagonals of the grid also contain every number from 1 to 9.

		9	4	1		7	6	3
				5	2			
		7		3	9	5	2	8
	2		5		4		8	6
	7		1		3	2	5	
	1			9			4	
				6	5			
						8	1	5

do you KNOW?

What is the definition of pharmacognosy?

_____

_____

LETTER LINE

Put a letter in each of the squares below to make a word that means "A PLACE OF STUDY."
The number clues refer to other words that can be made from the whole.

4 3 6 9 1 5 7 EXAMPLES OF MORAL EXCELLENCE • 7 1 6 4 5 10 INSPECT
4 5 3 2 7 TUBES • 9 1 2 5 6 7 DEVICES TO SELECT SIGNALS

1	2	3	4	5	6	7	8	9	10

TRIVIA QUIZ ## Sun, Moon, and Stars

Look to the sky for the answers to this astrological round.

1. What is the name of the Egyptian god of the sun?
   a. Ra
   b. Osiris
   c. Tut

2. Which rock musical featured the song "Good Morning Starshine"?
   a. Jesus Christ Superstar
   b. Tommy
   c. Hair

3. In *Star Wars Episode VI: Return of the Jedi,* which monstrous villain was choked to death by Princess Leia?
   a. Boba Fet
   b. Jabba the Hutt
   c. Admiral Ackbar

4. How many astronauts have walked on the moon?
   a. 39
   b. 7
   c. 12

5. Which country has a symbol called the Sun of May at the center of its flag?
   a. Argentina
   b. Greece
   c. Japan

6. In Greek mythology, whose wings melted when he flew too close to the sun?
   a. Hermes
   b. Icarus
   c. Prometheus

7. Who wrote the novel *The Moon and Sixpence?*
   a. Somerset Maugham
   b. Theodore Dreiser
   c. Aldous Huxley

8. Kenney Jones replaced Keith Moon in which pop group?
   a. The Oak Ridge Boys
   b. Pink Floyd
   c. The Who

9. Sun Myung Moon is the leader of what?
   a. South Korea
   b. The Unification Church
   c. Hyundai

10. Who starred in the 1954 version of *A Star Is Born?*
    a. Judy Garland and James Mason
    b. Marlene Dietrich and Mickey Rooney
    c. Doris Day and Rock Hudson

triVia • How much time does it take for sun rays to reach Earth?

Name That Beatles Tune!

ACROSS

1 Coffee cup holder
5 Yawning gulf
10 "Urgent!" on a memo
14 Narcissus spurned her
15 Tiki carver of New Zealand
16 Taboo
17 Commotion
18 Crack under pressure
19 In a frenzy
20 Mole passage
22 Moon of Saturn
24 Reverend famous for bloopers
26 Sired, Biblically
27 River of Poland
28 Lands
31 Publishing IDs
34 Inverts a stitch
36 It can be aroused
37 Give sparingly
38 Eeyore's creator
39 Mean mood
40 Memorable period
41 Piebald pony
42 Volcanic spillage
43 Capable of being cut
45 St. Paul's Cathedral designer
47 Odd fellows
48 "When I find myself in times of trouble …" song
52 Empire State capital
54 *Prozac* ____ (2001)
55 Floral rings
56 "… I'm forever in your debt" song
60 Queen Elizabeth II's daughter
61 Piquant
62 Stood up
63 Pour

64 Bookie's figures
65 Brewing need
66 Circular current

DOWN

1 Orange scrapings
2 Throw a scene
3 *Ice Age* heavy
4 "The day breaks, your mind aches" song
5 More plentiful
6 Shearing noise
7 Word after hither
8 Indian term of respect
9 "These are words that go together well" song

10 Like old watches
11 "You know I believe and how" song
12 At a later time
13 Elbow in the ribs
21 Eagle catchers?
23 Sponsorship
25 Plunderings
26 Screeching bird
29 Light haircut
30 Arista
31 "Beware the ____ of March!"
32 Seeing red
33 "Take these broken wings …" song

35 Last month: Abbr.
38 Earth's galaxy
39 Clean
41 Subatomic particle
42 Prefix for physics
44 "L'chaim" et al.
46 Milk curdler
49 Like pitchforks
50 Filleted
51 No friend
52 Female voice
53 Set the pace
57 Mined mineral
58 Extinct kiwi relative
59 Sancho's mount

Keep Going

Start on a blank square of your choice and connect as many blank squares as possible with one single continuous line. You can only connect squares along vertical and horizontal lines, not along diagonal lines. You must continue the connecting line up until the next obstacle, i.e., the border of the box, a black square, or a square that has already been used. You can change direction at any obstacle you meet. Each square can only be used once. The number of blank squares that will be left unused is marked in the upper square. There is more than one solution. We only show one solution.

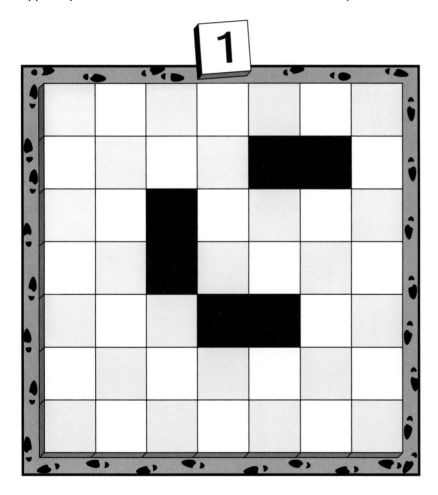

change ONE

Change one letter in each of these two words to form a common two-word phrase.

CAKE RACK

Kakuro

Each number in a black area is the sum of the numbers that you have to enter in the next empty boxes. The empty boxes that make up the sum are called a run. The sum of the across run is written above the diagonal in the black area, and the sum of the down run is written below the diagonal. Runs can only contain the numbers 1 through 9, and each number in a run can only be used once. The gray boxes only contain odd numbers and the white only even numbers.

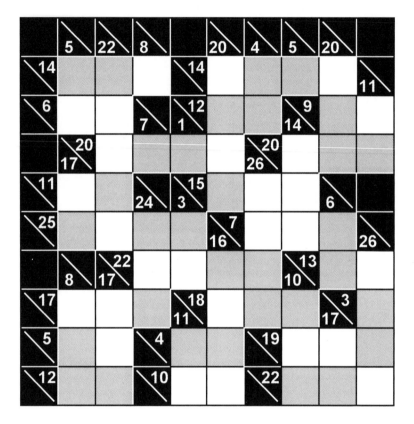

do you KNOW?

What famous novel is set in Thornfield Hall?

_____

_____

CROSSWORD # Presidential Losers

ACROSS

1 Marjoram, e.g.
5 It may need dusting
9 Men of wisdom
14 Director/producer Kazan
15 Arrowrock Dam's river
16 Rhone tributary
17 1936 loser to Roosevelt
19 Narrow groove
20 Sunburn aftermath
21 Take away from
23 Willow tree
25 Collation
26 Persuade
29 1957 Buddy Holly hit
33 Matchless
34 Secret observers
35 Swing to and ___
36 Kickoff shouts
37 One going downhill fast
38 Marinate
39 K-O connection
40 Rotates
41 Maestro Koussevitzky
42 One of these days
44 Comic Howie
45 The McCoys, for one
46 "Light My Fire" group
48 Spotted
51 Alberta expanse
55 Beyond angry
56 1800 loser to Jefferson
58 *The Tempest* sprite
59 Some are bagged
60 Encumbrance
61 Barry Manilow hit
62 Dull pain
63 Mana of tennis

DOWN

1 Trouble quantity?
2 Covergirl Macpherson
3 In widespread use
4 Swells up
5 Journalist Chung
6 Blue ___ Mountains
7 Spanish bear
8 Remain unresolved
9 *Hannah and Her* ___ (1986)
10 Off the path
11 1976 loser to Carter
12 "Layla" singer Clapton
13 Rush-hour subway rarity
18 Supermarket section
22 Kuwaiti royal
24 Kvetched
26 Sagan and Sandburg
27 Southwest poplar
28 2008 loser to Obama
30 Struggles
31 ___ *in Harlem* (1991)
32 Hayseed
34 No-fat milk
37 Lackey's lack
38 Well-thought-out
40 Majestic
41 Plastic wrap
43 Gleeful
44 Filled with gloom
47 Dr. Phil's mentor
48 Neeson in *Rob Roy*
49 Odd, in Dundee
50 Lab findings
52 Wrack's partner
53 All het up
54 Composer Dohnányi
57 DOE predecessor: Abbr.

Long before Microsoft brought us the Xbox, kids entertained themselves with these simple games and toys.

WHICH ONES DO YOU REMEMBER?

1 Sixty years ago, kids needed to supply their own spuds to play with this Hasbro offering.

_____

2 By 1958, kids could play with four colors of this modeling compound (blue, red, yellow, off-white) originally marketed as wallpaper cleaner.

_____

3 It bounces, stretches and settles into a blob if you leave it alone. And at one time kids used it to transfer graphics from the comic pages.

_____

4 Sales for Wham-O's gravity-defying spinning plastic rings were estimated at more than 100 million in 1958 alone.

_____

5 Five dice, one cup, one score pad, two pencils and 20 plastic chips came inside a box that touted this product as "the FUN game that makes THINKING...fun!"

_____

6 With eight oblong holes, this lightweight but tough plastic ball allowed children to play baseball in confined areas.

_____

7 First launched through FAO Schwarz, these flexible vinyl shapes were hand-cut and stuck like magic to a playboard.

_____

triVia • At age 14, who became the U.S. chess champion and at 15 became both the youngest grandmaster up to that time and the youngest candidate for the World Championship?

_____

WORD SEARCH **Bicycle**

All the words are hidden vertically, horizontally, or diagonally—in both directions. The letters that remain unused form a sentence from left to right.

```
C Y C L I S R A B E L D N A H
N T G C H A I N B L A D E I S
G E O O D D R U M B R A K E F
O K C O L R T Y O U R H E A L
C C T H P R L E B A S P U M P
A A R A E W N I A R U R A B L
R R E N A W C N R N E K O P S
B B N D H Y S O O I H N T K I
O I H E C E T I C E I T R Y G
N Y E L O C S U A O F O O T N
E L E N E N I D R E F M A E P
S C H L E S L T F R A M E T O
G Y F P E I C O Y N U R F U S
D E S K G P Y E Y B S T E O T
R U A H I E C D N A I T N R I
S R T R O D N F A S T K D E R
B T H A N A C O M P U T E R I
N T H G I L R A E R A C R A R
```

- BICYCLE
- BRACKET
- BRAKES
- CARBON
- CHAIN BLADE
- CITY BIKE
- COMPUTER
- CYCLISTS
- DRUM BRAKE
- DYNAMO
- FENDER
- FORK
- FRAME
- GEAR
- HANDLEBARS
- HEADLIGHT
- INNER TUBE
- LOCK
- PEDAL
- PUMP
- RAINWEAR
- REAR LIGHT
- REFLECTOR
- ROUTE
- SIGNPOST
- SPOKE
- SUSPENSION
- WHEELS

Circle of Color

In each of these puzzles, the aim is to draw lines linking the circles of like colors.
Sound easy? The difficult part is making sure that none of the lines crosses any other.

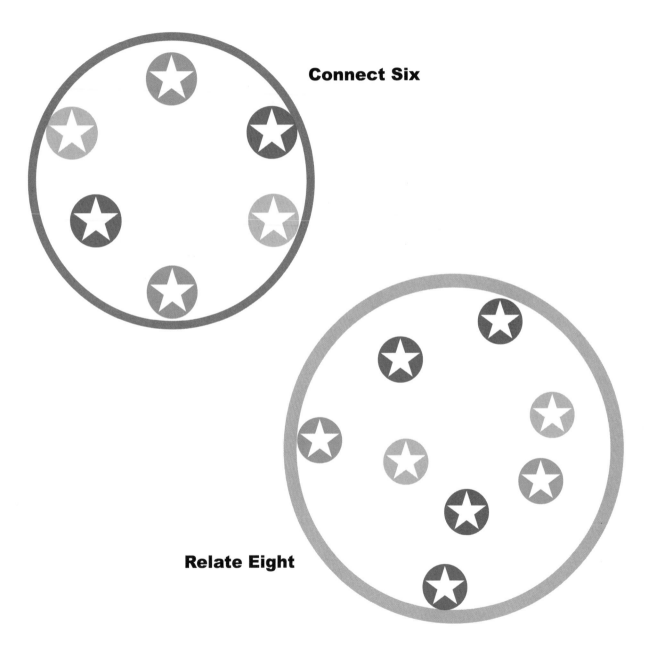

Connect Six

Relate Eight

Five to Five

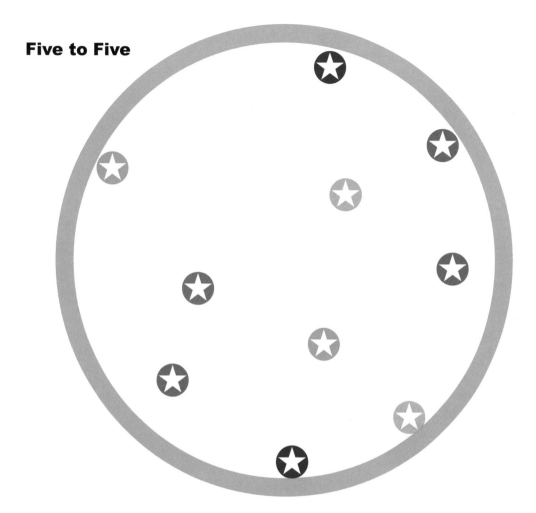

SANDWICH

What three-letter word belongs between the word on the left and the word on the right so that the first and second word, and the second and third word, each form a common compound word or phrase?

M A S S _ _ _ L E S S

Sudoku

Fill in the grid so that each row, each column, and each 3 x 3 frame contains every number from 1 to 9.

						2		6
	8						3	
	7			6	2		5	
	1				4			
8				2				
	3		6				8	2
			4	1	7	9		8
	6	7	2		5			1
1			3				2	

do you KNOW

Which Shakespeare play mentions America?

_____

_____

ONE LETTER LESS OR MORE

The word on the right side contains the letters of the word on the left side, plus or minus the letter in the middle. One letter is already in the right place.

G E N E R A T E +M **G** ☐ ☐ ☐ ☐ ☐ ☐ ☐

134

CROSSWORD Famous Arians

ACROSS

1 *The Good Earth* wife
5 Silicon Valley giant
10 Gothic arch
14 Big wheels for a big wheel
15 Weighted net
16 Bring up baby
17 Arian Renaissance man
20 *Terms of Endearment* heroine
21 Forgetfulness
22 *The Chill* detective Archer
24 Getz of jazz
26 Filled-pasta dish
30 Males with mail
34 Fail to name
35 Lopez in *The Dirty Dozen*
37 ABBA drummer Brunkert
38 Arian pontiff
42 Poetic for "before"
43 "Set Fire to the Rain" singer
44 Cambodian currency
45 Twine threads
47 Narrow swords
50 Fish with "wings"
51 "Seats sold out" sign
52 Hold back, as a story
55 USO show audience
60 Arian U.S. President
65 Dalai ___
66 Canton capital west of Zurich
67 On the Adriatic
68 *Shih Ching* verses
69 Get bent out of shape
70 Genie's home

DOWN

1 Pueblo cooking vessel
2 In ___ of (supplanting)
3 Companion of Venus
4 Taboo
5 Where shekels are spent
6 *Our Idiot Brother* brother
7 Padre's brother
8 Tom Brady's target
9 Grassy tract
10 Help get settled
11 Refined chap
12 Per capita
13 "Clinton's Folly" canal
18 He sang about Alice
19 Pickle brand
23 Testifier
24 Web designers?
25 Collette of *United States of Tara*
26 It's good to know them
27 Lifeless
28 Puff adder, e.g.
29 Suffix for London
31 Nerve, in slang
32 Tiny eel
33 Exemplar of toughness
36 Diminutive noun suffix
39 Smoothie fruit
40 Swirling water
41 Corn or angle starter
46 Kitchen emanations
48 Tricky
49 Skin orifice
52 City SE of Cherbourg
53 "___ no idea!"
54 "Bring It on Home ___": Cooke
56 Like courtroom testimony
57 Pelion's sister peak
58 "A ___ lovely as a tree": Kilmer
59 Crackle's colleague
61 Droop
62 Cyclist Ullrich
63 Roy Halladay stat
64 Out there

Futoshiki

Fill in the 5 x 5 grid with the numbers from 1 to 5 once per row and column, while following the greater-than/lesser-than symbols shown. There is only one valid solution that can be reached through logic and clear thinking alone!

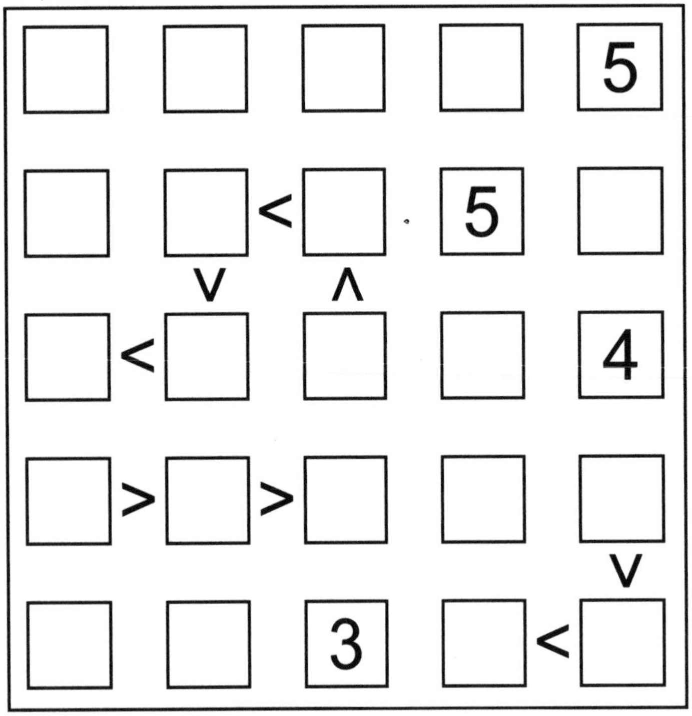

				5
	<		5	
	<			4
	>	>		
		3		<

(Row 2–3: ∨ below first blank, ∧ below the blank before 5)
(Row 4–5: ∨ above the last column)

trivia

- What are the names of Popeye's four nephews?

_____

_____

_____

_____

CONNECT TWO

An oxymoron is a combination of seemingly contradictory or incongruous words, such as "science fiction" (science means "knowledge or study dealing with facts or truth," while fiction means "an imagined or invented creation"). Connect the words with meanings that oppose each other and make oxymorons.

GLOBAL	**PREGNANT**
ALMOST	**VILLAGE**
FORGOTTEN	**WHISPER**
LOUD	**MEMORIES**

136

Word Sudoku

Complete the grid so that each row, each column, and each 3 x 3 frame contains the nine letters from the black box below. The hidden nine-letter word is in the diagonal from top left to bottom right.

E H I L O R S T X

							O	
		I				R		
								E
	E		X					
	L		I					H
T	H		L	O			S	
		H	R	L				
H	T	O			I			
R			T	E	X			

LETTERBLOCKS

Move the letterblocks around so that words associated with the environment are formed on the top and bottom rows.

More Wordplay

ACROSS

1 Aware of
5 It grows in the dark
10 Open, but barely
14 Picasso's room
15 Do more than apologize
16 James in *Only When I Laugh*
17 Invectives from the aft?
20 Backslide
21 Very vivid
22 Philippine volcano
23 Coffee tank
24 Highland plaids
28 Wordsmiths
32 Projecting window design
33 Ancient Roman senate
35 Wimbledon champ Seixas
36 Be inclined (to)
37 Blanches
38 Cleave
39 Some spaces
40 Taxonomic category
41 Candy nut
42 *She Done Him Wrong* star
44 Prickly plant
46 Echidna's morsel
47 Shady Tolkien creature
48 Isherwood's *The Berlin* ___
52 One of the Bee Gees
56 Note from Leo Burnett?
58 "Let's shake ___!"
59 "Guitar Town" singer Steve
60 "Small world, ___ it?"
61 Alongside of
62 Profound fear
63 Memo

DOWN

1 Stalin's empire
2 Chopped liver dish
3 Russian skater Protopopov
4 Did some voice-over work
5 Anglican preacher
6 SUVs
7 Soda
8 Cross letters
9 *Trinity* author
10 Stress
11 Dr. Dolittle
12 "Pocket rockets" in poker
13 Stage mom in *Gypsy*
18 Kathmandu locale
19 Heart parts
24 Pole carving
25 Orlando's Amway ___
26 Wash lightly
27 Hardly any
28 Gain by force
29 Give the boot
30 Beau number two
31 *CSI* center
34 Knife for Nanook
37 Wouldn't leave be
38 Hold back
40 Wish granter
41 Centerfold
43 Creature comfort
45 Off the disabled list
48 Garbage boat
49 Collette in *Little Miss Sunshine*
50 Bypass
51 Harry Potter ID mark
52 Powers in *The Storm Rider*
53 ___ facto
54 Wheatback coin
55 "Symphony in Black" artist
57 Rancor

WEATHER CHART **Sunny**

Where will the sun shine? With the knowledge that each arrow points to a place where a symbol should be, can you locate the sunny spots? The symbols cannot be next to each other, vertically, horizontally, or diagonally. A symbol cannot be placed on top of an arrow. We show one symbol.

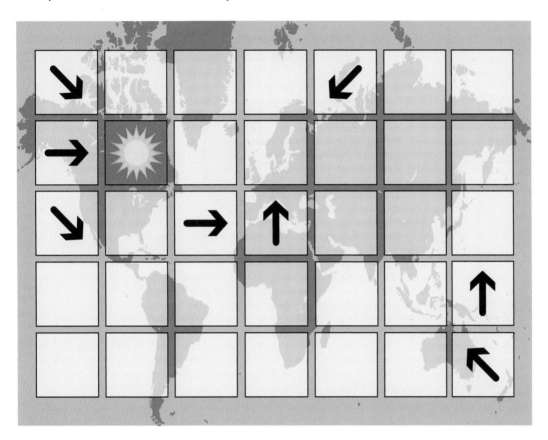

BLOCK ANAGRAM

Form the word that is described in the parentheses using the letters above the grid. An extra letter is already in the right place.

ICE BLISTER (widely known persons)

Curl It

Where (1–14) will yellow team's fourth curling stone come to rest?

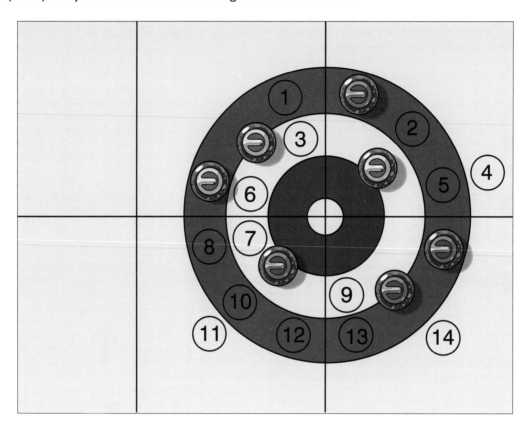

TRANSADDITION

Add one letter to **ARISE** and rearrange the rest to find a connection.

_____

TRIVIAL PURSUIT **1956**

From humble beginnings, Dean Martin, a suave crooner, and Jerry Lewis, a slapstick comedian, together hit their stride as comedy royalty. They were kings of comedy on stage and screen—and America's No. 1 box-office earners from 1950 to '56.

SEE WHAT YOU REMEMBER ABOUT THIS DROLL DUO.

1 What was Dean Martin's real name? Jerry Lewis' real name?

6 Name their first movie together.

2 Which one was born in the Midwest, and where?

7 The duo appeared as mystery guests on what game show in 1954?

3 Where did their act debut on July 25, 1946?

8 Name their last movie before they split in 1956?

4 Name the 1949 NBC radio show they hosted together.

9 Where was their farewell appearance?

5 What was the name of their televised variety show?

10 Who reunited the duo at the 1976 Muscular Dystrophy Telethon?

TEST YOUR RECALL

In 1956 what was the best children's TV series, and on what network did it air?

Screen Legends Said

ACROSS

1 Consequently
5 *Romeo and Juliet* et al.
10 Wooley in *Hoosiers*
14 Sign of decay
15 *Network* director
16 Tel Aviv dance
17 *Casablanca* heroine
18 Maternal relative
19 Big-budget film
20 "I never enjoyed working in a film": source
23 Tennis do-over
24 Curtail
25 Keene of Nancy Drew books
29 After the fact
33 Shangri-las
34 Toughen by exposure
36 Sugar suffix
37 Not on tape
38 Balsa vessels
39 Place Sundance liked
40 Wide shoe's letters
41 ___-burly
42 Whey-faced
43 Ammo
45 Renters
47 Lyricist Gershwin
48 Depot: Abbr.
49 "Big girls need big diamonds": source
58 Sarah Brightman, e.g.
59 Entrance courts
60 Captive of Hercules
61 Ways away
62 Culpability
63 Snowmobile
64 Patch up
65 Stadium path
66 New Mexico art colony

DOWN

1 Shipshape
2 Hawaiian skirt
3 Cold War superpower
4 *The Expendables* director
5 Oodles
6 Moon over Paris
7 *Diary of ___ Black Woman* (2005)
8 Sherpa bugaboo
9 2009 Super Bowl winners
10 Himalayan porter
11 Pueblo sun god
12 Rocker Burdon
13 One of the Three B's of music
21 Sushi seafood
22 Enameled metalware
25 Star
26 Bye-bye, in Burgundy
27 Paint the town red
28 Approaches
29 Inner tube rubber
30 Chilled ___ bone
31 Chandler or Lauder
32 College VIPs
35 Org. for 9 Down
38 Swedish turnip
39 Emerson, notably
41 Greek equivalent of Juno
42 *The Thin Man* dog
44 Chameleon, e.g.
46 Demesne
49 Netherlands cheese
50 Prison sentence
51 Cyclist Basso
52 Sewing case
53 Speaker of baseball
54 Sledding site
55 Germany's Oscar
56 Bread spread
57 Warren Beatty film

BRAINSNACK® **Fencing**

Which post (1–4) should replace the arrow?

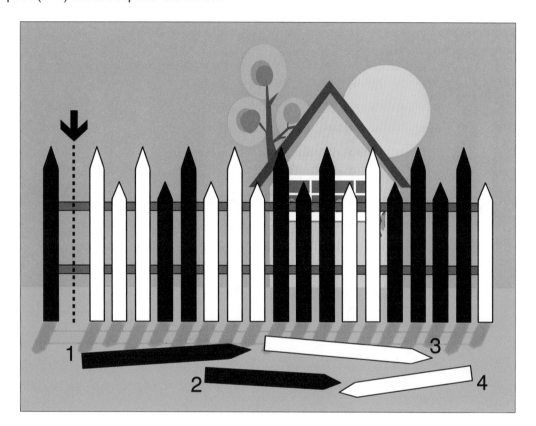

DOODLE PUZZLE

A doodle puzzle is a combination of images, letters, and/or numbers that represent a word or a concept. If you cannot solve a doodle puzzle, do not look at the answer right away. Think hard—and outside the box.

Sport Maze

Draw the shortest way from the ball to the goal. You can only move along vertical and horizontal lines, not along diagonal lines. The figure on each square indicates the number of squares the ball must be moved in the same direction. You can change direction at each stop.

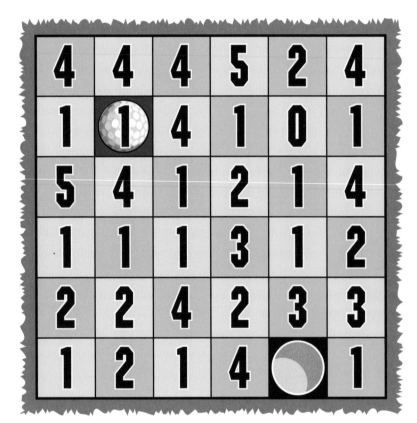

UNCANNY TURN

Rearrange the letters of the phrase below to form a cognate anagram, one that is related or connected in meaning to the original phrase. The answer can be one or more words.

NIGHT WANED

CROSSWORD Presidents Cup—U.S.A.

ACROSS

1 2011 Presidents Cup golfer
5 On the ball
10 Do without
14 To be, in French class
15 Synagogue scroll
16 Latvian capital
17 Shrinking sea of Asia
18 Black wood
19 Living legend
20 2011 Presidents Cup golfer
22 Gumbo pod
23 Homo sapiens, e.g.
24 *Spamalot* creator Eric
26 Danson of *CSI*
27 Single guy
31 Cuban leader
34 Windows font
35 Road sign
36 Laundry unit
37 Mini
38 Churn up
39 Off-road vehicle
40 Preppy jackets
41 Lane in a Beatles song
42 Denied
44 Goldilocks was found in one
45 Judge
46 Otitis
50 Spy Hari
52 2011 Presidents Cup golfer
55 Ancient lyre
56 University founder Yale
57 ___ de force
58 Hammock support
59 In the sticks
60 Noted *Harper's Bazaar* artist
61 Child's play
62 Tuscany city
63 Owner's certificate

DOWN

1 Track trials
2 Anchors aweigh position
3 O'Hara's ___ *to Live*
4 Picked
5 Drunk as a skunk
6 Freight train hoppers
7 Ending with buck
8 Cape Town coin
9 Touchy-feely
10 Camden Yards bird
11 2011 Presidents Cup golfer
12 *The Munsters* bat
13 River to the Indian Ocean
21 Cambodian currency
25 Global shipping company
27 Rancher's mark
28 Is bedbound
29 *Chocolat* actress Lena
30 ___-poly
31 Jolly Roger, for one
32 Teensy bit
33 2011 Presidents Cup golfer
34 "Help," in Tours
37 Stutters
38 Edited
40 112.5 degrees heading
41 Home to El Misti volcano
43 At hand
44 Scott in *American Beauty*
46 *Fargo* producer Coen
47 A piece of work
48 ___ cuisine
49 Goofed
50 Lion with a mane
51 Global area
53 His, in Caen
54 Pirelli product

Trick-or-Treat

All the words are hidden vertically, horizontally, or diagonally—
in both directions.

- COSTUMES
- LANTERN
- SUPERSTITION
- FANTASY
- FACE PAINT
- PUMPKIN
- CARAMEL
- PRANK
- SCARE
- SPOOKY
- BLACK CAT
- BATS
- HAUNTED HOUSE
- NIGHT
- DOORBELL
- MONSTER
- CANDY
- SPIDER WEB
- BOO
- FRIGHTEN
- TREAT BAG
- HALLOWEEN
- CAULDRON
- MASK

```
F V O H E L V V B Q S V C V A S Y X T
A L P P D O O R B E L L E U D J A G N
N V R A G H O H L A B E L K K R P S P
T W C I E A Z G A K T N V W J M M C R
A B A T Q L S E M U T S O C R N C E A
S Y R Q Q L G O Z H N I P H B W J U N
Y T A U Y O A J N N F T J S D A U W K
T Y M O B W B Q O G T R E A I J G B B
Z S E B S E T M I B N N I D X A P V C
R I L H C E A P T V E O I G H E S U A
J E T D A N E J I R E W R A H O N W N
Z S A L R K R Y T A E I R D P T U D D
E W C A E Y T G S Z A T K E L E E S Y
M P K N T K D O R E Y R S E D U C N E
X N C T L O R O E D V E G N D I A A D
L I A E R O J O P O S X K P O V P C F
P G L R M P Y B U T B H A E C M R S B
E H B N K S Q G S P P U M P K I N O Y
P T C I B E A N Y K S A M V G X L P F
```

Sudoku

Fill in the grid so that each row, each column, and each 3 x 3 frame contains every number from 1 to 9.

1			8					
4							5	
			9	6		7		
			3					
		9			6			7
			7			8	2	3
		8		9		5		
2	6	3				4	1	9

do you KNOW?

What part of the flower is the corolla?

_____

_____

ONE LETTER LESS OR MORE

The word on the right side contains the letters of the word on the left side, plus or minus the letter in the middle. One letter is already in the right place.

D E C E A S E D -E ☐ ☐ ☐ A ☐ ☐ ☐

Directors Said

ACROSS

1 Hole makers
5 Rough sketch
10 Wide-spreading trees
14 Stew vegetable
15 Fuel ship
16 Floor model
17 Roman 1052
18 Florida orange center
19 Andean ancient
20 "Drama is life with the dull bits cut out": source
23 Word form for "bad"
24 Toddler
25 Said one's lessons
29 Bow down before
33 Store up
34 Millennium's 1,000
36 ___ pro nobis
37 Supersonic speed unit
38 Pharmacy stock
39 For men only
40 Casino area
41 Related to the kidneys
42 Where the action is
43 On the skids
45 Like romantic nights
47 "Disgusting!"
48 Fjord cousin
49 "I dream for a living": source
58 Elbe tributary
59 *Silver Shark* novelist Andrews
60 Skullcap's lack
61 Frosty coat
62 Kind of hockey
63 Needlepoint fabric
64 Forcibly dislodge
65 Thompson and Samms
66 English prep school

DOWN

1 *Brokeback Mountain* heroine
2 Place for wishing
3 Explorer Ericson
4 Minor battle
5 Scribble
6 High in calories
7 Jai ___
8 Pool table cloth
9 Farm vehicles
10 Public notices
11 Letterman's rival
12 Nero's 2200
13 Linger in the hot tub
21 Chuckwagon offerings
22 ___ d'oeuvre
25 Highway exits
26 Electronic message
27 Flora in the Mojave
28 Faulkner's *As I Lay* ___
29 "If these ___ could talk …"
30 "Monopoly" purchase
31 Native of Tabriz
32 Brewster of *Criminal Minds*
35 Guido's note
38 Whittling tool
39 Board game with letters
41 Risotto ingredient
42 Participate in America's Cup
44 Detour
46 Sneaker bottoms
49 Manhattan art gallery district
50 "How Great ___ Art"
51 Years of note
52 Willowy
53 "The Bells" is one
54 *Lost ___ Mancha* (2002)
55 Part of QED
56 Puerto ___
57 FBI agents

TRIVIA QUIZ # Parks for Grown-ups

Maybe you've visited some of these parks; maybe you haven't. Can you still identify them?

1. North America's highest mountain is located in which national park?

_____

2. Which national park in Kentucky contains the world's largest-known cave?

_____

3. Which park served as an internment camp in World War II?

_____

4. What does the Golden Spike National Historic Site in Utah commemorate?

_____

5. In which park do alligators and crocodiles exist side by side?

_____

6. In which state can you find Smokey Bear Historical State Park?

_____

7. The Women's Rights National Historic Park marks the site of the first women's rights convention. Where is it?

_____

8. Cadillac Mountain and Mount Desert Island call which park home?

_____

9. What is the most visited national park?

_____

10. In which state would you find Petrified Forest National Park?

_____

11. Where is Canyonlands National Park located?

_____

12. Which state is home to the Appomattox Court House National Historical Park?

_____

13. In which state would you find Guadalupe Mountains National Park?

_____

14. Do you really know where you are when you visit Yellowstone National Park? Name the three states that play host to it.

_____

Keep Going

Start on a blank square of your choice and connect as many blank squares as possible with one single continuous line. You can only connect squares along vertical and horizontal lines, not along diagonal lines. You must continue the connecting line up until the next obstacle, i.e., the border of the box, a black square, or a square that has already been used. You can change direction at any obstacle you meet. Each square can only be used once. The number of blank squares that will be left unused is marked in the upper square. There is more than one solution. We only show one solution.

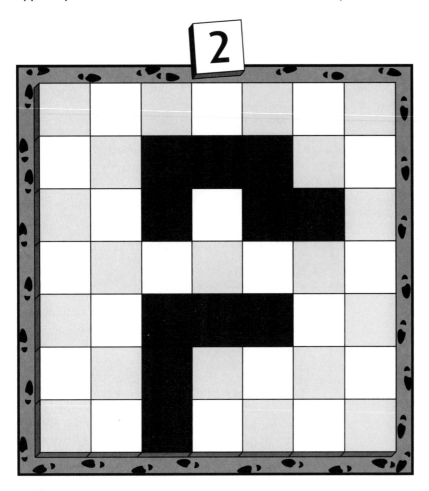

delete ONE

Delete one letter
from
HIRE CANDLES
and find another
light source.

CROSSWORD Presidents Cup—International

ACROSS

1 One doing impressions
5 Off-the-cuff remark
10 Taj Mahal site
14 Prefix with scope
15 Hindu trinity member
16 Given by
17 Word after he and she
18 Encrypted
19 Cabinet face-lift
20 2011 Presidents Cup golfer
22 Important periods
23 Cannes movie house
24 Take hold
26 Ridiculous
29 Cruet contents
32 Twin crystal
33 Made a choice
34 Chromatin component
35 Dull pain
36 Dental filling
37 Self-satisfied
38 Mrs. bear
39 Like the Indian elephant
40 Blinding light
41 Photobucket upload
43 *A Few Good Men* director
44 Pitcher's mound bag
45 Salve
46 Catcher's glove
48 2011 Presidents Cup golfer
52 Thick goo
53 Easy ___
55 Aussie leaper
56 Wilson in *Midnight in Paris*
57 Charlie Bucket's friend
58 Gush forth
59 Shaker contents
60 "... ___ of skimble-skamble stuff": Shak.
61 Lick and stick

DOWN

1 Church recess
2 Tree for a partridge
3 Activist Brockovich
4 Mock
5 Balloon up
6 Asian wild dog
7 Kettle covers
8 "___ Got My Eyes on You"
9 2011 Presidents Cup golfer
10 Shaking in one's shoes
11 2011 Presidents Cup captain
12 Cabbed it
13 "Winter" singer Tori
21 Tipperary locale
24 Darkness Prince
25 Dollop
26 Stockpile
27 Side with eggs
28 2011 Presidents Cup golfer
29 Hitting sound
30 Make accustomed to
31 Amber ale
33 Salsa ingredient
36 2011 Presidents Cup golfer
37 Model quality
39 Pack animal
40 1996 Peace Prize Nobelist
42 Packing a wallop
43 Varlet
45 Rum cake
46 Jersey sounds
47 Home of the Hawkeyes
48 Miss Marple
49 Trick
50 Region
51 Mournful cry
54 Turf

Honey Cell

Which cell (1–31) should be filled with honey?

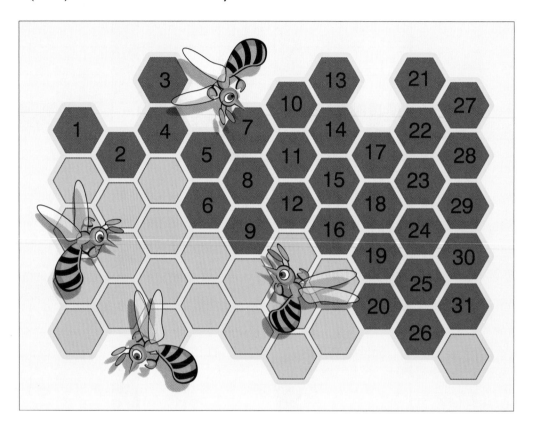

TRANSADDITION

Add one letter to **TRAFFIC RULE** and rearrange the rest to find a connection.

_____

Binairo

Complete the grid with zeros and ones until there are 5 zeros and 6 ones in every row and every column. No more than two of the same number can be next to or under each other. Rows or columns with exactly the same content are not allowed. There is only one valid solution.

		1								
							1			
1		1	1				1		0	
	1									
					1				1	
	1		1	1					1	
			1		1		1			
		0				0	1			
			0							
			0		0	0			0	
	0	0							0	

do you KNOW

What insect was Napoleon's official emblem?

_____

_____

SANDWICH

What five-letter word belongs between the word on the left and the word on the right, so that the first and second word, and the second and third word, each form a common compound word or phrase?

S T A G E _ _ _ _ _ L I N E

Webster Says Not 1

ACROSS

1 Sand at Augusta
5 Young herring
10 Caps
14 Suffix with soft or hard
15 Share knowledge
16 Uzbekistan sea
17 Got riled up
18 Zellweger in *Leatherheads*
19 Chest sound
20 War room gathering?
23 Some are rainy
24 Pool temperature tester
25 Trace
26 Corkscrews
31 Tooth type
34 Seabirds
35 By birth
36 Deep blue
37 Found out
38 End of a 12/31 song
39 Antique auto
40 Aches
41 *A Tramp Abroad* author
42 Game in which one knocks
44 "Annabel Lee" poet
45 Id, it's not
46 Penny Marshall TV role
50 Mount Holyoke vis-à-vis Napa Valley College?
55 Film director Kazan
56 Inedible orange
57 Scarlett O'Hara's daughter
58 Smaller amount
59 Speak
60 Pants section
61 Walkway
62 Clairvoyants
63 Newcastle river

DOWN

1 Leafless branches
2 Peep show
3 Sports site
4 Bust site
5 Pearl collection
6 Prepares a banana
7 Bullfrog genus
8 Waldo Pepper et al.
9 Stephen King novel
10 Impaired
11 Quick horse
12 Like John Isner
13 Loom reed
21 Big noise
22 Eternities
26 Like title roles
27 Overthrows first
28 "Storms in Africa" singer
29 "Madonna of the Rosary" artist
30 Visualized
31 Helgenberger of *CSI*
32 "The ___ Love": R.E.M.
33 Penn State mascot
34 Kind of life insurance
37 Funny
38 Most saccharin
40 Quite significant
41 "L'Shana ___" (Rosh Hashanah greeting)
43 Tread old ground
44 Harness horses
46 Olympic sledder
47 Life of ___ (ease)
48 *The Dark Knight* director
49 Related to mom
50 Beatles movie
51 Jejunum neighbors
52 Essential point
53 Renaissance patron
54 See socially

TRIVIA QUIZ Storied Creatures

How much do you know about these much-loved animal
characters from children's literature?

1. What sort of animal is Hairy Maclary?

   a. Dog
   b. Llama
   c. Gorilla
   d. Tarantula

2. What were Flopsy, Mopsy, and Peter?

   a. Animated table settings
   b. Butterflies in *Beauty and the Beast*
   c. Earthworms
   d. Rabbits

3. Which type of creature was Beatrix
   Potter's Mrs. Tiggy-Winkle?

   a. Hedgehog
   b. Giraffe
   c. Bat
   d. Robin

4. In *Alice in Wonderland*, who was having
   tea with the Mad Hatter and the dormouse
   when Alice arrived?

   a. Spring chicken
   b. June bug
   c. March hare
   d. White rat

5. What sort of animal is Winnie the Pooh's
   friend Eeyore?

   a. Ostrich
   b. Warthog
   c. Ogre
   d. Donkey

6. According to the nursery rhyme, what did
   Mary have?

   a. A little lamb
   b. A little pony
   c. A little turkey
   d. A little cat

7. What is the name of Doctor Dolittle's
   parrot?

   a. Cracker
   b. Rainbow
   c. Polynesia
   d. Polly

8. Which character was surprisingly cowardly
   in *The Wizard of Oz*?

   a. The scarecrow
   b. The lion
   c. The flying monkey
   d. The tin man

9. What was the name of the Darling family's
   dog in *Peter Pan*?

   a. Nana
   b. Sparky
   c. Scottie
   d. Manfred

10. In *The Jungle Book*, what sort of animal
    was Baghera?

    a. A cow
    b. A vulture
    c. A panther
    d. A bear

Number Cluster

Cubes showing numbers have been placed on the grid below, with some spaces left empty. Can you complete the grid by creating runs of the same number and of the same length as the number? So, where a cube with number 5 has been included on the grid, you need to create a run of five number 5's, including the cube already shown. The run can be horizontal, vertical, or both horizontal and vertical.

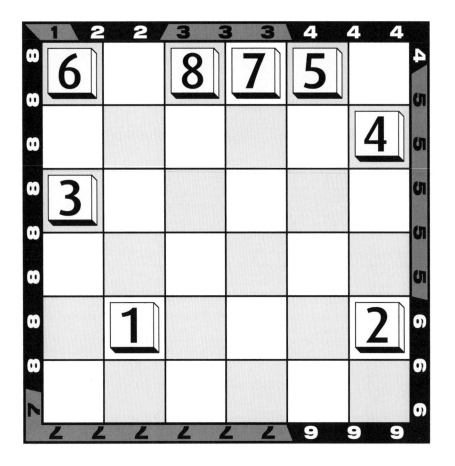

do you KNOW?

Who had a No. 1 hit with "Shadow Dancing"?

FRIENDS

What do the following words have in common?

SCHOLAR WORKMAN CENSOR GUN READER

WORD SEARCH Social Contact

All the words are hidden vertically, horizontally, or diagonally—in both directions. The letters that remain unused form a sentence from left to right.

B Y B D O O F L N P A T U R M
Y L O O H C S E O H U D U U M
R A N B J H E I N V A O S G S
A S H O P I A S D N E I R F C
R E G A L L I V C R C E I G O
B N E C P D R E H T E G O T F
I H C F A R L I N C E D T O F
L O I A R E L I V O E G W E E
I B F M T N E V E L Y N V T E
H B F I N H S E N L S I I L T
H Y O L E G I A E E E D V I H
I O T Y R U H N C C Y D F S C
O R S T H A O T E T E E N T U
E P O P U L A R R E I W D E O
S O F M I E M A B I E V R N T
N O I T A T I V N I B S I O F
V I S I T N A T H M E E T T E
I R S G I F T L O C I E T Y Y

ACTIVITY
BIRTH
CHILDREN
COFFEE
COLLECT
DANCE
EVENT
FAMILY
FOOD
FRIENDS
GIFT
GROUP
HOBBY
HOSPITAL
INVITATION
JOB
LAUGH
LIBRARY
LISTEN
LONELY
LOVE
MEET
MUSIC
OFFICE
PARTNER
POPULAR
RECEIVE
SCHOOL
SHOP
TOGETHER
TOUCH
TRAIN
VILLAGE
VISIT
WEDDING

Sudoku Twin

Fill in the grid so that each row, each column, and each 3 x 3 frame contains every number from 1 to 9. A sudoku twin is two connected 9 x 9 sudokus.

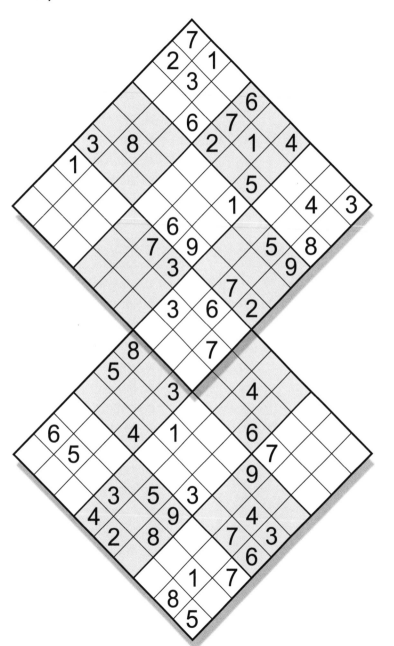

doubletalk

Homophones are words that share the same pronunciation, no matter how they are spelled. If they are spelled differently, then they are called heterographs.

Find heterographs meaning:

APTITUDE and
A RESCUE ROCKET

_____

_____

◄►

CROSSWORD Webster Says Not 2

ACROSS

1 Creamy dressing
6 Nonsense poet
10 Talking horse
14 Great Plains hub
15 Knight's wreath
16 "I see," facetiously
17 Animal with a flexible snout
18 Minnesota NHL team
19 Bona fide
20 Remote possibilities?
22 Necessitate
24 Hard to pin down
25 Eldest daughter of Laban
26 Tennis star who wrote *Open*
29 Scold sharply
33 Areas between shoulders?
34 Charlatan
35 Q-Tip
36 Of the ear
37 Eye makeup
38 Boxy transports
39 Bag of chips, say
40 Signs a contract
41 Pig out
42 Super Bowl I winners
44 "Imagine" singer
45 Lewis or Sandburg
46 "The King" of soccer
47 New Englander
50 Japanese dish
54 Third of thrice
55 2011 Kenneth Branagh film
57 Nasal cavity
58 Dog's warning
59 Schlep
60 Like water from a well
61 "A miss ___ good as a mile"

62 Belgian river
63 "___ one" (ticket notation)

DOWN

1 Campus cadet org.
2 *The Joy Luck Club* nanny
3 Mondavi Winery locale
4 Shanghai cloakroom attendants?
5 Trotter's gear
6 Humble
7 Sister of Ares
8 *In toto*
9 Deliverer
10 Stewart's grand cru?
11 Poseidon's mom
12 Morales of *Caprica*
13 Barbie, for one
21 Yalie
23 Catch red-handed
25 Michigan and Ontario
26 Tag ___ with (accompany)
27 Everglades critter
28 Absinthe ingredient
29 Spare and tall
30 NFL Hall-of-Famer Lynn
31 Dance for two
32 *Barnaby Jones* star Buddy
34 Last test
37 Opera text
41 "Summer Rain" singer Carlisle
43 Scots negative
44 Albanian coin
46 Baby food
47 Bear or Berra
48 Sothern and Jillian
49 Hall of Champions org.
50 Barflies
51 Director Avakian
52 Fruit with green pulp
53 "Send in the Clowns" starter
56 ___ polloi

Cookies

Which icing cookie (1–5) should replace the question mark?

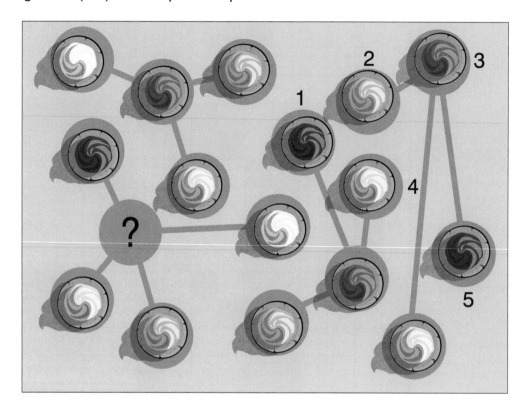

Word Sudoku

Complete the grid so that each row, each column, and each 3 x 3 frame contains the nine letters from the black box below. The hidden nine-letter word is in the diagonal from top left to bottom right.

D E I L N S T V X

E		X					
	X	I				N		
L	S						D	
D						I		
	E		N					
			D			T	X	
	L			V	I	D	N	
	N	D	S			V	L	
			I				E	

do you KNOW?

Which instrument has keys, pedals and strings?

_____

_____

LETTERBLOCKS

Move the letterblocks around so that words associated with artists are formed on the top and bottom rows.

Big Words 2

ACROSS

1 Inform the host
5 Full
10 Pronto!
14 Mimic
15 Florida *CSI* setting
16 ___ San Lucas
17 Having large feet
19 The yoke's on them
20 Flapjacks
21 Pauline's problems
23 Evened the score
24 Retired French coin
25 Jog the memory
28 Flourishes
31 Belch
32 Desire
33 Back muscle, briefly
34 Floor decor
35 Pontificate
36 Kind of chest
37 Caesar's 250
38 Salty imperative
39 Abdul or Cole
40 Glabrous
42 Filmed
43 Clockwork, mostly
44 Byron or Tennyson
45 Vampire repellent
47 Cajole
51 His, to Henri
52 The symbol #
54 Plunders
55 Eurasian elk
56 Substance
57 Geoffrey of *Shine*
58 Caught morays
59 *Enchanted* Hathaway role

DOWN

1 Coarse file
2 Pet welfare org.
3 Band of gold
4 It makes perfect
5 Like Virginia ham
6 Lent support to
7 New Mexico tourist town
8 Five-foot-tall bird
9 Refute
10 Squirrel's stash
11 Growing among rocks
12 First fratricide victim
13 Coloratura Lily
18 Primer, for one
22 Make bearable
24 Lester of bluegrass
25 Gag
26 Durance of *Smallville*
27 Ill temper
28 Military leaders
29 Syrup source
30 Lieu
32 Crude
35 Defeat
36 Like Apollo
38 Half a Basque game
39 W Australia capital
41 Enjoy with gusto
42 Hit high
44 Freewheeling
45 Teri in *Oh, God!*
46 Baseball brothers
47 Plane for limited runways
48 City on the Oka River
49 "C'mon, be ___!"
50 Animal-rights org.
53 Track rival of Ovett

BRAINSNACK® Olives

Which group of three olives should replace the question mark above the lettered olives?
Answer like this: BDD.

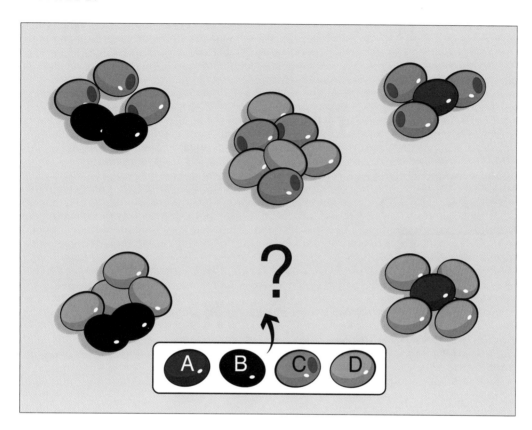

REPOSITION PREPOSITION

Unscramble **CANOE FLIP** and find a triple-word preposition.

_____

History Tour

The historian has already visited castles A, B and C. Which castle (1–9) will he visit next?

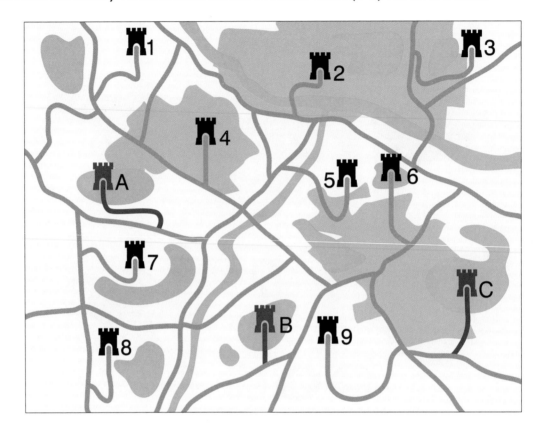

DOODLE PUZZLE

A doodle puzzle is a combination of images, letters, and/or numbers that represent a word or a concept. If you cannot solve a doodle puzzle, do not look at the answer right away. Think hard—and outside the box.

WORD POWER Misused?

We've polled a long list of writers and editors to gather words often misused, misspelled, or misunderstood. Here are some common offenders.
How will you fare (not to be confused with *fair*)?

. . . .

1. **pallet** ('pa-luht) *n.*—A: roof of the mouth. B: painter's board. C: makeshift bed or portable platform.

2. **sophomoric** (sahf-'mor-ik) *adj.*—A: philosophical. B: immature. C: inducing sleep.

3. **secede** (sih-'seed) *v.*—A: achieve one's goals. B: withdraw. C: come next after.

4. **accede** (ak-'seed) *v.*—A: surpass or overcome. B: agree. C: manage to reach.

5. **jalousie** ('ja-luh-see) *n.*— A: window blind. B: envy. C: dilapidated car.

6. **prevalent** ('pre-vuh-luhnt) *adj.*— A: widespread. B: first in line. C: seeing the future.

7. **imminent** ('ih-muh-nuhnt) *adj.*— A: outstanding. B: about to happen. C: inborn.

8. **aural** ('or-uhl) *adj.*—A: of the ears. B: of the mouth. C: faintly glowing.

9. **collegial** (kuh-'lee-jee-uhl) *adj.*— A: very courteous. B: relating to a college. C: marked by camaraderie among colleagues.

10. **bellwether** ('bel-'we-thur) *n.*— A: trend leader. B: church spire. C: balmy conditions.

11. **climactic** (kliy-'mak-tik) *adj.*— A: of prevailing weather. B: reaching a pause. C: at a decisive moment.

12. **impetus** ('im-puh-tuhs) *n.*— A: sterility. B: force, impulse, or stimulus. C: logical conclusion.

13. **emigrate** ('eh-muh-grayt) *v.*— A: leave one's residence or country. B: enter a country for permanent residence. C: illegally cross a border.

14. **incredulous** (in-'kre-juh-luhs) *adj.*—A: amazing, extraordinary. B: skeptical. C: ungrateful.

15. **venial** ('vee-nee-uhl) *adj.*— A: dishonest. B: unimportant. C: of the blood.

Weigh It Up

Which weight between 1 and 10 grams cannot be weighed with the three available weights using only one weighing?

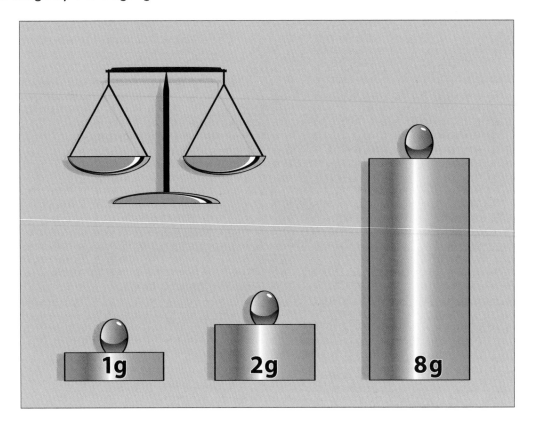

TRANSADDITION

Add one letter to MEASUREMENT and rearrange the rest to find a connection.

CROSSWORD **Celebrity Chuckles**

ACROSS

1 Classic song by the Kinks
5 Early Iranian
9 Unwanted mail
14 Gossipy twosome
15 Concluded
16 Ryan in *Barry Lyndon*
17 "Monopoly" rollers
18 "Do, ___, fa, sol ..."
19 It may make the cut
20 Hard sugar for a biting wit?
23 Poker great Phil
24 Windburned
25 Scalawag
28 Bar order
30 Chapel seat
33 Like royal jelly
34 Scrupulously avoid
35 Deep cut
36 Home to a woman of letters?
39 Joule fractions
40 Ache
41 More under the weather
42 ___ Anne de Beaupré
43 Stopping action on a ball
44 Water nymph
45 Michael Caine's title
46 Added stipulations
47 Comic's gallows jokes?
54 Of a zone
55 *Doctor Zhivago* heroine
56 "___ a Gal I Love": Sinatra
58 *Fiddler on the Roof* matchmaker
59 A party to
60 Honduras port
61 Rob of *90210*
62 Watch over
63 Succor

DOWN

1 Can cover
2 Narc ending
3 Poland's Walesa
4 2011 Presidents Cup winners
5 Bit of gossip
6 "___ Breath You Take": Sting
7 Test-drive car
8 "Flying Scotsman" Liddell
9 Wild feline
10 Not a blood relative
11 Unfatty
12 *Saigon* star Alan
13 Weaver's reed
21 The Donald's ex
22 Danish currency
25 Four-star reviews
26 Here and there?
27 Lightly burn
28 Bilbo Baggins' home
29 Jabba the ___
30 St. ___ Girl beer
31 German steel city
32 What place?
34 Bolted
35 *The Vicar of Wakefield* novelist
37 Go around and around
38 Adherent of the Vedas
43 Books from the Gideons
44 Let go
45 Oceanic ray
46 Ohio college town
47 Singer ___ P. Morgan
48 *Iliad* warmonger
49 One-___ sale
50 Settled down
51 Split rattan
52 Double curve
53 Lucky streak
57 Light knock

Tennis Players

All the words are hidden vertically, horizontally, or diagonally—in both directions. The letters that remain unused form a sentence from left to right.

S A R P M A S T O I D U A G E
T N N U I U S O R I G I N A G
E T E D S I S K I E F E R N N
P G I L B E R T E N G L A A G
A G A S S I D N E D A H S N R
N S D H A S B S L R C I E E E
E E H N P L A C K E T Y T O B
K E D E I N O I T I N F S R D
N A L B A N D I A N A D C N E
B V O N N L T L E R M P L E O
E R E O A A U P O R T A S C R
C Y R D F R O R B L A K E M M
K S A H E W I T T E S C A S H
E N K G I V N C E C T H E E N
R I O S D O D F T O G H E N I
N K R A J I C E K N E R T E E
R E D N A L I W M T N T O H C
E N A T F E D E R E R U R B Y

- AGASSI
- ASHE
- BECKER
- BLAKE
- BORG
- CASH
- CHANG
- CONNORS
- EDBERG
- FEDERER
- GAUDIO
- GERULAITIS
- GILBERT
- HEWITT
- KIEFER
- KORDA
- KRAJICEK
- LECONTE
- LENDL
- MCENROE
- MEDVEDEV
- MUSTER
- NADAL
- NALBANDIAN
- PORTAS
- RAFTER
- RIOS
- RUSEDSKI
- SAMPRAS
- STEPANEK
- WILANDER

Sudoku

Fill in the grid so that each row, each column, and each 3 x 3 frame contains every number from 1 to 9.

					3			
	8		9		2			
1		4						
		5	4					3
9			3			7		
	3							6
		3	1			4		
	9			2	8		3	
	5						6	8

do you KNOW?

Which European city was originally called Lutelia?

_____

_____

ONE LETTER LESS OR MORE

The word on the right side contains the letters of the word on the left side, plus or minus the letter in the middle. One letter is already in the right place.

D E C I M A L S +P ☐ I ☐ ☐ ☐ ☐ ☐ ☐

Nobility

ACROSS

1 Ellipsoidal
5 Gregorian ___
10 Little League stats
14 Honduran seaport
15 Roberts of *Fawlty Towers*
16 Stallion's supper
17 Crushed underfoot
18 Really shine
19 BBC viewer
20 Did the bidding of
22 Carve in relief
24 Not so rosy
26 Alice B. Toklas' friend
27 Moderately slow tempo
30 U2 guitarist
33 Overcharge
34 Gypsy's deck
36 ___ gratia artis
37 "My Way" lyricist
38 Martin in *Bobby*
39 Spacewalks
40 Glacier substance
41 *Moonstruck* song (with "That's")
42 Israel's chief port
43 Settled snugly
45 In need of a drink
47 Oft-bitten things
48 It's yelled on Wall Street
49 Poppycock
51 Houston hoopster
55 Went on horseback
56 First track, often
60 Earthenware pot
61 State point-blank
62 From Oslo
63 Oil burner
64 Graceful water bird
65 Texas breakfast choice
66 Book of Mormon book

DOWN

1 Dr. Octavius in *Spider-Man 2*
2 Action word
3 Burn balm
4 "Poker Face" singer
5 Things are bought on it
6 Put a jinx on
7 RSA political party
8 Before marriage
9 PBS fundraiser
10 *My Three Sons* son
11 He became a Cavalier in 2011
12 "That's the Way ___": Dion
13 Concordes
21 Northern Ireland river
23 Confront
25 Approaches
26 Local map lines
27 Now and ___
28 Present purpose
29 Ebbets Field center fielder
31 Political funny business
32 History class assignment
35 ___ Lingus airline
38 ___ salts
39 *Survivor: Fiji* winner
41 Shepard's ___ *of the Mind*
42 Hawaiian city
44 Place to throw darts
46 Champions
49 "Oh, phooey!"
50 Amble
52 Ku Klux ___
53 Roper of the polls
54 Military funeral sound
57 Neither here ___ there
58 Prefix for cycle
59 Q–U links

Spot the Differences

Find the nine differences in the image on the bottom right.

 do you KNOW?

What is the artist Picasso's first name?

_____

_____

trivia

- How many legs does a butterfly have?

_____

BRAINSNACK® Symbolism

Which symbol (1-6) should replace the question mark?

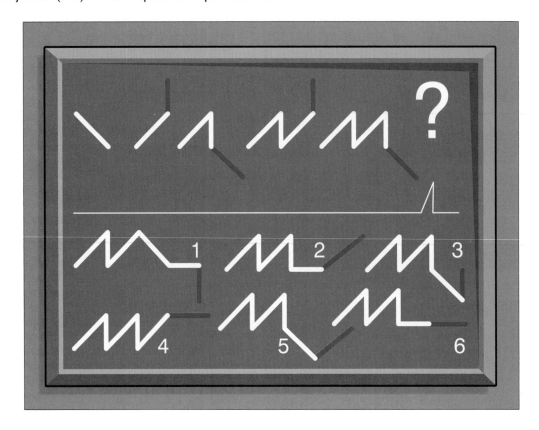

DOODLE PUZZLE

A doodle puzzle is a combination of images, letters, and/or numbers that represent a word or a concept. If you cannot solve a doodle puzzle, do not look at the answer right away. Think hard—and outside the box.

CROSSWORD Funny Ladies

ACROSS

1 Lyft competitor
5 1970s kidnapping victim Patty
11 Crock
14 Wander
15 Morphinelike drug
16 Spanish gold
17 Funny lady married to George Burns (2 wds.)
19 Smart _____ whip (2 wds.)
20 Alleviated
21 Between Aug. and Oct.
22 Pesky bug
23 Cola
26 Asparagus piece
28 Pokes at
31 Ahead of _____ time
33 Oak Ridge Boys song
36 Poem of tribute
37 Chunk
39 Cut
40 Pecans and almonds
42 Funny lady _____ Burnett (pictured)
44 Actor Jared
45 Singer John, known for his big eyeglasses
47 Epic tale
48 Edge
49 Fashions
51 Egg producer
52 On a ship
53 You swim in it
55 365 days
57 *The Wizard of Oz* actor Bert
59 Garfield, for one
61 *War and Peace* has 1,225
65 Who _____ to say? (2 wds.)
66 Well-loved funny lady (2 wds.)
69 Portable bed
70 Stadiums
71 "Woe _____!" (2 wds.)
72 Squeeze (out)
73 _____ breakfast (2 wds.)
74 Two peas in _____ (2 wds.)

DOWN

1 Desire
2 Word, repeated, is a Pacific island
3 Gabor and Marie Saint
4 Playtime at school
5 Gardener's tool
6 Ecological govt. agcy.
7 Feels poorly
8 Labored breaths
9 Russian grassland
10 Number of fingers
11 Funny lady who often filled in for Johnny
12 _____ Major or Minor
13 Animal that mows lawns
18 Wedded words
22 A judge wields one
24 It may be slipped in your back
25 Book with Africa and Australia
27 Raised-track trains (abbr.)
28 Monkees' singer Davy
29 Grown-up
30 Funny lady and Golden Girl (2 wds.)
32 _____, *Plain and Tall*
34 Lace up again
35 Scent
38 One over par
41 Powered by the sun
43 Memory or fast
46 Fishing tackle need
50 Safe
52 *Lawrence of* _____
54 Competed on a track
56 King Kong was one
57 Decorative stitching
58 Run _____
60 *Gilligan's Island* actress Louise
62 Express shock
63 *Sesame Street* character
64 Winter toy
66 Science room
67 Computer link (abbr.)
68 Hallucinogen (abbr.)

Keep Going

Start on a blank square of your choice and connect as many blank squares as possible with one single continuous line. You can only connect squares along vertical and horizontal lines, not along diagonal lines. You must continue the connecting line up until the next obstacle, i.e., the border of the box, a black square, or a square that has already been used. You can change direction at any obstacle you meet. Each square can only be used once. The number of blank squares that will be left unused is marked in the upper square. There is more than one solution. We only show one solution.

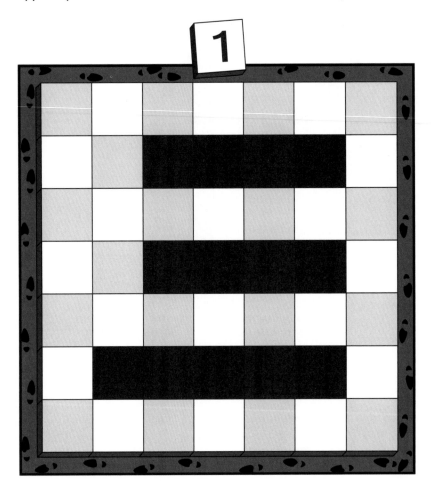

1

change ONE

Change one letter in each of these two words to form a common two-word phrase.

ALOUD WINE

TRIVIA QUIZ **Winning Colors**

Most sports are not for the color-blind. Here's a warm-up round that requires you to consider all the color details an athlete should know.

1. In which sport do red and yellow balls oppose black and blue balls?

   a. Croquet
   b. Polo
   c. Table pool

2. In which Canadian city do the Blue Jays play their home baseball games?

   a. Montreal
   b. Vancouver
   c. Toronto

3. Which English soccer team is nicknamed the Black Cats and plays its home games at the Stadium of Light?

   a. Sunderland
   b. Newcastle United
   c. Norwich City

4. What color belt does a first Dan wear in judo?

   a. Yellow
   b. Black
   c. Purple

5. What color is the center of an archery target?

   a. Black
   b. Red
   c. Gold

6. Which color is representative of the most difficult ski runs?

   a. Red
   b. Black
   c. Orange

7. Which colorful horse won the 2001 Grand National?

   a. Red Marauder
   b. Blue Angel
   c. Midnight Hero

8. What color shirts are worn by the French national rugby team?

   a. Blue
   b. Red
   c. Black

9. Which color is associated with the baseball teams of Boston and Cincinnati?

   a. Blue
   b. Red
   c. White

10. What color jersey did soccer goalkeeper Lev Yashin always wear when playing for Russia?

   a. Black
   b. Red
   c. Yellow

11. What color flag indicates a foul throw in a javelin competition?

   a. Yellow
   b. White
   c. Red

12. What color cap does a goalkeeper wear in water polo?

   a. Red
   b. White
   c. Orange

Themeless

ACROSS

1 Bryn ___ College
5 Impish one
10 "___ Hear Music": Beach Boys
14 Word form for "field"
15 Where James Bowie died
16 Gossip maven Barrett
17 Former Mets stadium
18 German pistol
19 Book of Mormon book
20 Like male models
22 "Dear" friend
24 Do the mall
25 "___, With Love": Lulu hit
26 Spielberg's "go"
29 Outerwear item
32 Taxi driver in *Taxi*
33 Heath shrub
34 West in *My Little Chickadee*
35 "*Dies* ___ " (Requiem Mass hymn)
36 Inscribed
37 Kindle ___
38 32,000 ounces
39 Karpov's game
40 Incendiarism
41 Like Pollock's art
43 *District 9* prawns
44 Album insert
45 Greek house
46 Grade of beef
48 Doc Brown's dog
52 Cologne address
53 Phileas Fogg's creator
55 Kathryn of *Law & Order: CI*
56 Scraps of food
57 Great Lakes tribesmen
58 Sheepskin leather
59 Mosquito, e.g.

60 South African coins
61 Recovering from surgery

DOWN

1 Radar's show
2 Ottoman Empire VIP
3 House bird
4 Billboard locale
5 Judge Roy Bean's "court"
6 Grass cluster
7 Opera singer Haugland
8 M.'s partner
9 Victim of a drift net
10 Double-edged

11 Give and take
12 Kournikova of tennis
13 It gets pounded
21 "Beat it, gnat!"
23 Ye olde Anglo-Saxon serf
25 Mini-pies
26 *The Red Tent* author Diamant
27 St. John's bread
28 Conveys
29 Henhouse perch
30 Hank who hit home runs
31 They're coming of age
33 Choreographer José
36 "It doesn't matter"

37 Apple doughnuts
39 Comfy shoe
40 "What a pity!"
42 Something to quench
43 James of *Gunsmoke*
45 Penalized
46 Take an ax to
47 Roll response
48 Ireland
49 Switch attachment?
50 Structural beam
51 Leakes of *TRHoA*
54 Mesozoic, e.g.

Futoshiki

Fill in the 5 x 5 grid with the numbers from 1 to 5 once per row and column, while following the greater-than/lesser-than symbols shown. There is only one valid solution that can be reached through logic and clear thinking alone!

			4	
2				
		>		
3	<			
		<		>

trivia

- Which Spice nickname did Geri Halliwell have?

_____

_____

CONNECT TWO

An oxymoron is a combination of seemingly contradictory or incongruous words, such as "science fiction" (science means "knowledge or study dealing with facts or truth," while fiction means "an imagined or invented creation"). Connect the words with meanings that oppose each other and make oxymorons.

ANXIOUS	**SHRIMP**
JUMBO	**SHADE**
LIGHT	**PILOT**
AUTO	**PATIENT**

Football Greats

These masters of the gridiron all got their start playing college football.
Do you know them well enough to trace each player back to his early beginnings?

1. Which quarterback for the Pittsburgh Steelers started his college career for Louisiana Tech?

   a. Roger Staubach
   b. Ken Stabler
   c. Terry Bradshaw
   d. Joe Namath

2. Which infamous running back for the Buffalo Bills played for the University of Southern California?

   a. Earl Campbell
   b. O. J. Simpson
   c. Franco Harris
   d. Walter Payton

3. Which tight end for the Oakland Raiders played for Notre Dame?

   a. Dave Casper
   b. Charlie Sanders
   c. Jim Langer
   d. Mike Webster

4. Which linebacker for the Chicago Bears first played for Illinois?

   a. Jack Lambert
   b. Dick Butkus
   c. Bobby Bell
   d. Jack Ham

5. Which defensive tackle for the Los Angeles Rams first played for Utah State?

   a. Merlin Olsen
   b. Alan Page
   c. Bobby Lilly
   d. Joe Greene

6. Which cornerback for the San Francisco 49ers first played for UCLA?

   a. Jimmy Johnson
   b. Roger Wehrli
   c. Louis Wright
   d. Willie Brown

7. Which fleet-footed running back for the Arizona Cardinals started his career playing college football for Miami?

   a. Edgerrin James
   b. Tim Castille
   c. Tim Hightower
   d. Joe Namath

8. Which Colts quarterback played college football for Tennessee?

   a. Jeff George
   b. Jim Harbaugh
   c. Peyton Manning
   d. Charlie Daniels

9. Which quarterback from the Philadelphia Eagles first soared in his college days at Syracuse?

   a. A. J. Feeley
   b. Kevin Kolb
   c. Donovan McNabb
   d. Boomer Esiason

10. Which Tampa Bay quarterback first played for San Jose State?

   a. Bruce Gradkowski
   b. Jeff Garcia
   c. Brad Johnson
   d. Jerry Garcia

VERBAL SKILLS Kissing Cousins

Match each word with its synonym by writing a number next to each letter.

. . . .

Kissing Cousins #1

1. Settle   ____a. Resist

2. Entreat   ____b. Compromise

3. Acquiesce   ____c. Grave

4. Dismiss   ____d. Coarse

5. Peevish   ____e. Wander

6. Vulgar   ____f. Enlarge

7. Rome   ____g. Petulant

8. Oppose   ____h. Implore

9. Amplify   ____i. Ignore

10. Solemn   ____j. Comply

Kissing Cousins #2

1. Egotism   ____a. Evasiveness

2. Grateful   ____b. Rugged

3. Approach   ____c. Fixed

4. Rough   ____d. Overstate

5. Immobile   ____e. Unwavering

6. Imitate   ____f. Vainglory

7. Secrecy   ____g. Vanquished

8. Exaggerate ____h. Advance

9. Persistent   ____i. Mirror

10. Conquered ____j. Appreciative

MLB Mascots

ACROSS

1 "This weighs ___!"
5 Cryptographic
10 Prig
14 Decorate freshly
15 ___ and beyond
16 Blanchett in *Notes on a Scandal*
17 Deplaned, e.g.
18 Principle
19 Plugging away
20 Ace's team
22 Take great pleasure in
24 Semiotics study
25 Silent *Duck Soup* star
26 Woman in Lennon's "Woman"
27 Isinglass
28 Rajon Rondo's org.
31 *Hannah Montana* character
34 Lou Seal's team
36 Huffington Post buyer
37 Plumber's tool
39 Throw on the floor
40 Jock's wife in *Dallas*
42 TiVo ancestor
43 Black suit
46 Land in the sea
47 University conferral
48 Chapeau carrier
49 Grey Cup stats
51 Albertville river
53 Bureaucratic bind
57 From Odense
59 Southpaw's team
60 New York cardinal
61 Exceedingly
63 Africa's longest river
64 Standout
65 Pamphleteer of 1776
66 River through central Germany
67 Miss on the brae

68 The Witch House site
69 What's remaining

DOWN

1 Fiery horses
2 British boob tube
3 Abhorrence
4 Dell product
5 L.L. Bean mailing
6 Does what a good dog does
7 Knotts and Adams
8 Garden party?
9 Divert
10 Charge a fortune
11 Screech's team
12 Williams of the Temptations
13 Sister of Meg, Jo, and Amy
21 Operatic tenor Vickers
23 Remove from the board
25 Bivalve joint
27 Norman Lear sitcom
29 Be plenty hot
30 Away from the wind
31 "Answer, please"
32 Make a small move
33 Fredbird's team
35 Ready to blow one's top
38 Selleck's *Blue Bloods* costar
41 He's all ears
44 "If you play your cards right"
45 NOW founder Gloria
50 Former insecticide
52 Nasal congestion locale
53 Bonn river
54 Stage whisper
55 Ends of the earth
56 Use energetically
57 "The Farmer in the ___"
58 Oaxaca water
59 Mimic a banshee
62 Ovine sound

WORD SEARCH **Public Transportation**

All the words are hidden vertically, horizontally, or diagonally—in both directions. The letters that remain unused form a sentence from left to right.

```
A N I A R T D E E P S H G I H
C O M P A N Y R I K L C K S H
A W A R T K O I N D I A O F B
I C F R O Y Y I C L E R C T A
T X A I R T A A T N D A T O M
I M R O E R C W U A N T A S L
M B E L G E E U L E T A N H I
E P D M N V Y G D I A S C L C
T A O N E I B T I N A A E C C
A O D T S R N S I O O R I D O
B N G E S D J R E C N C D A N
L S I A A S F U E O R A R M N
E F N G P U U G N Y O E L F E
P A G U H B A B B C A L T I C
T R A I N T I C K E T L C N T
L E U F S T B R A N S I E P I
L A P I C I N U M O R T O D O
A T I O T R A N S F E R N N N
```

- BUS DRIVER
- BUS STOP
- COMPANY
- CONDUCTOR
- CONNECTION
- DELAY
- FARE
- FARE-DODGING
- FUEL
- HIGH-SPEED TRAIN
- INTERCITY
- JUNCTION
- LOCAL
- MUNICIPAL
- NIGHT BUS
- PASSENGER
- RAILWAY
- REGIONAL
- STAGE-COACH
- STATION
- STRIKE
- TIMETABLE
- TRAIN TICKET
- TRAM
- TRANSFER

Sudoku

Fill in the grid so that each row, each column, and each 3 x 3 frame contains every number from 1 to 9.

			9					
	5							
		3	2			6		
			8	7				
3		5		6		8		
	7			2	3		5	9
6		9	5	8	1		4	
5	2			4				
7	4			9		3	8	5

do you KNOW?

What is the common name for ascorbic acid?

_____

_____

ONE LETTER LESS OR MORE

The word on the right side contains the letters of the word on the left side, plus or minus the letter in the middle. One letter is already in the right place.

| B | E | D | R | O | O | M | S | -S | | O | | | | |

CROSSWORD Capital Namesakes

ACROSS

1 School mil. program
5 Speedway sound
10 Antiquing device
14 Aviating prefix
15 Prefix with structure
16 Pother
17 Get ___ a good thing
18 One getting stuffed
19 Corey in *The Lost Boys*
20 Ontario city*
22 Like a runway model
24 Sicilian summer resort
26 Instead of
27 Copyist
29 Indiana's "Lake City"*
32 Not true
33 With merriment
35 "By what means?"
37 Source of pollen
38 Kicks out of office
39 Are in the past?
40 Tumult
41 Desired guests
42 Chicago airport
43 Moves obliquely
45 Personify
47 Beehive state
48 Disquiet
49 Border town of
   northern New York*
52 Van Zandt of *The
   Sopranos*
56 By mouth
57 Cul-___ (dead-end
   street)
61 Corona
62 Zachary of *Chuck*
63 Shelley's Muse
64 Some van Goghs
65 Arabian Sea gulf
66 Get *Mad* again
67 Lea Michele series

DOWN

1 Racetrack fence
2 Wine prefix
3 2010 Disney film
4 Abbreviate
5 Washington, D.C.
   suburb*
6 Cytoplasm component
7 Frequently, to Byron
8 Valuable strike
9 Fugitive hunters
10 City in Georgia*
11 Hockey score
12 Polish a draft
13 Central New York city*
21 Generous offer
23 Modify
25 Misery
26 A social network
27 City in NE Texas*
28 1985 film set in Greece
30 *The Road* ___: Bill Gates
31 "What, me ___?": Alfred
   E. Neuman
32 Big name in bouquets
34 Jerk
36 Mini
38 Janet Fitch's *White* ___
39 All the way
41 Tenor's higher-up
42 A few last words?
44 Columbus, Ohio suburb*
46 Idaho border city*
49 *Shark Tale* dragon fish
50 Riled up
51 Lay away
53 Rockies resort
54 Blonde in *Legally Blonde*
55 Muzzle
58 Before
59 ___ Quentin
60 Suffix for emir

Americana

From the land that gave birth to baseball,
Budweiser, and bebop, we bring you this homegrown mix of
words, phrases, and names.

· ·

1. **pompadour** ('pahm-puh-dohr)
   n.—A: parade uniform.
   B: convertible top. C: men's
   hairstyle.

2. **El Capitan** (ehl 'kahp-ee-'tahn)
   n.—A: Alamo general. B: Yosemite
   rock formation. C: Civil War
   stronghold.

3. **jackalope** ('jak-uh-lohp) *n.*—
   A: rabbit with antlers. B: rodeo
   bronco. C: crusading journalist.

4. **barnstorm** ('barn-storm) *v.*—
   A: travel around performing.
   B: dance at a hoedown.
   C: give a ranting speech.

5. **ponderosa** (pahn-deh-'roh-suh)
   n.—A: gold mine. B: pine tree.
   C: mountain range.

6. **fake book** ('fayk book) *n.*—
   A: recipe folder or container.
   B: stack of marked playing cards.
   C: collection of songs.

7. **tricorn** ('try-korn) *adj.*—
   A: popped, as in kernels.
   B: deliberately campy.
   C: like Paul Revere's hat.

8. **bunting** ('buhn-ting) *n.*—
   A: fabric for flags. B: baby boy.
   C: Roaring Twenties dress.

9. **Tin Pan Alley** (tihn pan 'a-lee)
   n.—A: hideout for hoboes. B: row
   of factories. C: pop music center
   formed in the late 19th century.

10. **twain** ('twayn) *n.*—A: disguise.
    B: male suitor. C: two.

11. **moxie** ('mahk-see) *n.*—
    A: chorus girl. B: courage.
    C: double-talk or deceptive
    message.

12. **brushback** ('bruhsh-bak) *n.*—
    A: grooming technique for a
    horse. B: baseball pitch.
    C: method of sawing or logging.

13. **eighty-six** ('ay-tee 'siks) *v.*—
    A: round up. B: get rid of.
    C: submerge.

14. **copacetic** (koh-puh-'seh-tik)
    adj.—A: very satisfactory.
    B: satirical. C: pepped up.

WEATHER CHART — **Sunny**

Where will the sun shine? With the knowledge that each arrow points to a place where a symbol should be, can you locate the sunny spots? The symbols cannot be next to each other, vertically, horizontally, or diagonally. A symbol cannot be placed on top of an arrow. We show one symbol.

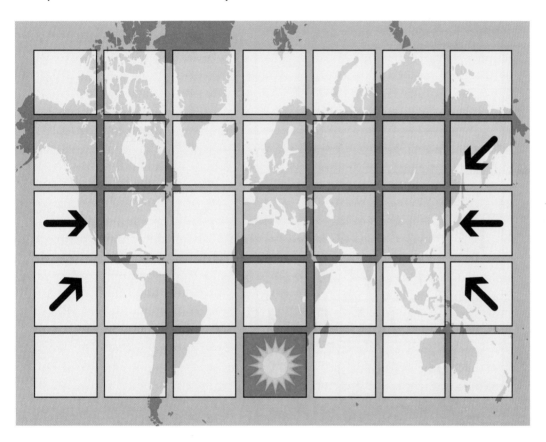

BLOCK ANAGRAM

Form the word that is described in the parentheses using the letters above the grid. Extra letters are already in the right place.

PROTESTER (police officer)

Word Sudoku

Complete the grid so that each row, each column, and each 3 x 3 frame contains the nine letters from the black box below. The hidden nine-letter word is in the diagonal from top left to bottom right.

E H I L M P R S U

E	H			P	I			
	U							
		M			L			
	R							
M			I	E	P			
				U		H	I	
S					U	I	P	H
L				M				R
					E			

do you KNOW

Which sea does the Jordan River flow into?

_____

_____

LETTERBLOCKS

Move the letterblocks around so that words associated with herbs and spices are formed on the top and bottom rows.

G	O	O	R	A	E	N
R	P	A	A	I	P	K

186

CROSSWORD Crooners

ACROSS

1 Catch, as a sweater
5 Makes up on the spot (2 wds.)
11 Plead
14 Actress Skye of *Say Anything*
15 Buddy Holly played it
16 Eggs
17 Crooner who left his heart in San Francisco (2 wds.)
19 Part of a drill
20 Fix a mistake
21 Short for emotional
22 Partner of ready and willing
23 Greek god of love
26 Like a mountain peak
28 Gene Kelly's prop in *Singin' in the Rain*
32 Actor James of *The Blacklist*
35 Exercise, _____ chi
36 Beige
38 Madrid's Museo del ____
39 Coffee containers
41 Crooner Sinatra
43 Morphine, for example
44 Opposite of wrong
46 Cut back a plant
48 Diamonds nickname
49 Iridescent layers
51 Vertical mesh used to catch fish (2 wds.)
53 Actress Zellweger
55 A Great Lake
56 Opposite of bad
58 Tire pressure measurement (abbr.)
60 Fresher
64 Passport and driver's license (abbr.)
65 Crooner who sang "Mona Lisa" (3 wds.)
68 Watch chain
69 Where you may wear your heart
70 *The Tender _____*, 1955 Debbie Reynolds film
71 Make an effort
72 Analyzes
73 Longings

DOWN

1 Location
2 Jordanian queen
3 _____ *and the King of Siam*, 1946 movie
4 Yellowstone feature
5 _____ of consent
6 Grayish brown
7 Johnny Cash walked it
8 The parts in a set
9 They get twirled
10 Abbr. in many Dodge cars
11 Crooner who sang "Splish Splash" (pictured, 2 wds.)
12 Wicked
13 A fence door
18 French-style hat
22 Grammy or Tony
24 St. _____ College, MN
25 Drink noisily
27 Same antonym (abbr.)
28 Change direction 180 degrees
29 Main character in *The Sound of Music*
30 Crooner who sang "White Christmas" (2 wds.)
31 Separate
33 Call to mind
34 He wrote a thesaurus
37 Harden
40 Tear up
42 Knot in a tree trunk
45 Perfect score
47 J.R. of *Dallas*
50 Parts of flowers
52 Fort Myers location (2 wds., abbr.)
54 _____ Park, CO
56 Talent
57 Smell
59 Swedish multinational
61 Had on
62 Enthusiasm
63 Salespeople (abbr.)
65 Similar to the CIA
66 _____ League, oldest colleges
67 Early gaming console (abbr.)

Word Wheel

How many words of three or more letters, each including the letter at the center of the wheel, can you make from this diagram? No plurals or conjugations. We've found 18, including one nine-letter word. Can you do better?

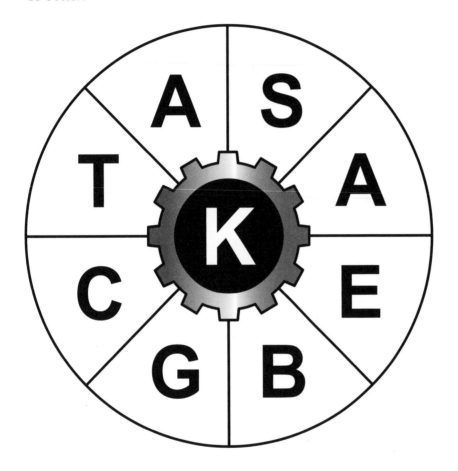

- _____
- _____
- _____
- _____
- _____
- _____
- _____
- _____
- _____
- _____
- _____
- _____
- _____
- _____
- _____
- _____
- _____
- _____

trivia

- Who had the hit "Bette Davis Eyes" in 1981?

WORD SEARCH **Shipping**

All the words are hidden vertically, horizontally, or diagonally—in both directions. The letters that remain unused form a sentence from left to right.

```
A S U E Z C A N A L B I T L E
S S T R E N I A T N O C H K P
A N S N F R I G A T E I C I N
T E T A R O H C N A Y O H P E
P R O V I S I O N S L S A I L
R H O R E L L E P O R P F C E
N I Y P R T O O F A I N E R E
C N A N T E E R W R D I R E S
A E W N A M P C T R I A R K U
R B R O A N A E A A L T Y N O
G A E S W N E O E O R P L A H
O R T D O G B P D W T A R T T
S G A E D R I A D E S C E S H
H E W E A L O C C U P E R A G
I S R T O V I A S H I R N G I
P D S T R E K N A T L I O I L
P P P A N A M A C A N A L T M
I N G L A N D I N G C R A F T
```

- ANCHOR
- CANOE
- CAPTAIN
- CARGO SHIP
- CONTAINER
- DREDGE
- FERRY
- FRIGATE
- GAS TANKER
- LANDING CRAFT
- LIGHTHOUSE
- LOCK
- MAST
- MINESWEEPER
- OIL TANKER
- PANAMA CANAL
- PILOT
- PORT
- PROPELLER
- PROVISIONS
- RHINE BARGE
- SAIL
- SAILOR
- STARBOARD
- SUEZ CANAL
- TORPEDO
- WARSHIP
- WATERWAY

The Play's the Thing

ACROSS

1 CBS eye, e.g.
5 Colorful lizard
10 Doctor of afternoon TV
14 Color similar to flax
15 Silky synthetic
16 Ward in *Almost Golden*
17 "In a cowslip's bell I lie." play
19 Phillips University city
20 Latticework
21 Battened down
23 Suffering from dementia
24 Macbeth or Gaga
25 Unless, in law
27 "Mellow Yellow" singer
30 Sees eye to eye
33 Faucet issues
35 Wall Street newbie: Abbr.
36 Minstrel songs
37 Society's finest
38 Skewbald
39 Hurler's pride
40 Bread spreads
41 Nullifies
42 Lexicographer Noah
44 Leap ___
46 Cast-of-thousands film
47 When tulips bloom
51 Actress Flockhart
54 Impassive
55 Classical Roman poet
56 "My kingdom for a horse!" play
58 Christmas tree
59 Dimwit
60 Neuter a horse
61 "... happily ___ after."
62 Hindu social class
63 Limerick language

DOWN

1 Riga natives
2 Earth tone
3 Shrek's color
4 Preliminary sketches
5 Mailer's ___ *of the Night*
6 Fissures
7 Popeye's assent
8 Trunk growth
9 Gazelle
10 Fake
11 "Press not a falling man too far!" play
12 "Should ___, madam?": Shak.
13 Alan in *Shane*
18 Couturier Perry
22 Recyclable items
26 Wastrel
27 Lightheaded
28 Parodied
29 "Yes" signals
30 Nitpicker's find
31 Swiss waterway
32 "Hath Britain all the sun that shines?" play
34 Brazil cruise stop
37 Like the Tesla Roadster
38 What Goldilocks ate
40 Driftwood in *A Night at the Opera*
41 Contrail
43 Miss Muffet's scarer
45 Big house
48 Slicker
49 They grow on you
50 Ride the updrafts
51 Manage all right
52 Tel ___
53 Verdi opera
54 Scotch measure
57 ___ *for Corpse*: Grafton

BRAIN FITNESS # Train Your Brain

Take a look at the sets of images below. Your task is to deduce which of the four options given in each case completes the set.

Jumping for Joy

A

B

C

? D

Find the Flag

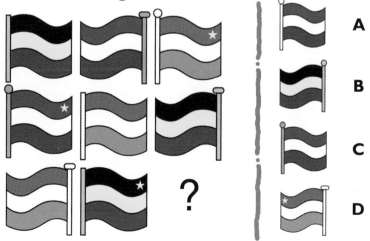

A

B

C

? D

Sudoku X

Fill in the grid so that each row, each column, and each 3 x 3 frame contains every number from 1 to 9. The two main diagonals of the grid also contain every number from 1 to 9.

2		4	1			5		3
	9		2			1	6	8
6			8		5		9	
9	5				8			
	1		7				4	
			9					
						7	5	9
			4		3			
		8						

do you KNOW?

Which country was named after Venice?

_____

_____

LETTER LINE

Put a letter in each of the squares below to make a word that means "A MEMBER OF THE ALCEDINIDAE FAMILY." The number clues refer to other words that can be made from the whole.

4 10 2 9 5 SORROW • 8 2 3 4 9 JOINT
5 10 2 7 1 QUICK SEARCH • 5 9 2 4 3 PRETEND

1	2	3	4	5	6	7	8	9	10

Sport Maze

Draw the shortest way from the ball to the goal. You can only move along vertical and horizontal lines, not along diagonal lines. The figure on each square indicates the number of squares the ball must be moved in the same direction. You can change direction at each stop.

4	2	4	4	2	3
1	1	4	1	2	⬤
4	4	1	3	1	4
4	3	1	2	1	5
1	1	4	4	2	2
3	3	5	4	1	4

do you KNOW?

What does SFX represent in film and advertising?

_____

_____

UNCANNY TURN

Rearrange the letters of the phrase below to form a cognate anagram, one that is related or connected in meaning to the original phrase. The answer can be one or more words.

RATE MY LIFE

Choose Your Cheese

The mouse has already collected four cheese cubes. Which cheese cube (1–6) will it collect now?

REPOSITION PREPOSITION

Unscramble **DREAM IF SO** and find a two-word preposition.

_____

CROSSWORD Weather-Wise

ACROSS

1 Guinness in *The Detective*
5 Third-stringer
10 Dame Everage
14 Minderbinder in *Catch-22*
15 Seismograph detection
16 Necessity
17 Markedly similar
18 Incited
19 Decorative arch
20 Fan undulations at Miami NBA games?
22 Feline murmurs
23 The Old Sod
24 Former Genoese magistrate
25 Pain in the neck
28 ___ pike
32 Deep-felt
33 Worker's incentive
34 Scooby-___
35 Criminal charges
36 MLB commissioner Bud
37 Stereotypical hobo apparel
38 Paris–Lyon direction
39 Bluegrass partner of Scruggs
40 Check recipient
41 Harry Potter's friend
43 Swanson in *The Phantom*
44 Batman's hideaway
45 "Super!"
46 Sexologist Hite
48 Unfriendly facade?
53 Steersman's station
54 SE Asian capital
55 Gravelly ridges
56 Column part
57 Newark's "The Rock" is one
58 Utah ski resort
59 Like today, tomorrow
60 Jacobi in *I, Claudius*
61 Toontown judge

DOWN

1 Far East nurse
2 Relish
3 Astronomer Millosevich
4 Matches
5 Checkerboard space
6 Parabola
7 Fashion craze
8 Hula instruments
9 Lake floor
10 *The World Is Not* ___ (1999)
11 Commencement times?
12 ___-do-well
13 Field drinks
21 Sly stratagem
22 Chef's equipment
24 Merck product
25 Like Siberian winters
26 "___ of do or die ..."
27 Smartphones, e.g.?
28 Nick in *Warrior*
29 "Get___!" ("Start working!")
30 Noted thesaurian
31 Meddlesome
33 Lima or pinto
36 Fruity gin flavoring
37 B&O, for one
39 Till bill
40 Faculty member
42 Rockies rodent
43 Alaskan bear
45 Dolly the sheep, e.g.
46 Boutique
47 Sister of Zeus
48 Concern
49 Rare person
50 Kon-Tiki Museum site
51 The Spanish call it OTAN
52 Streetcar
54 Taken advantage of

Kakuro

Each number in a black area is the sum of the numbers that you have to enter in the next empty boxes. The empty boxes that make up the sum are called a run. The sum of the across run is written above the diagonal in the black area, and the sum of the down run is written below the diagonal in the black area. Runs can only contain the numbers 1 through 9, and each number in a run can only be used once. The gray boxes only contain odd numbers and the white only even numbers.

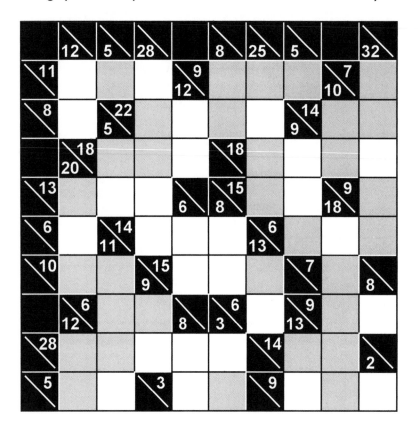

do you KNOW?

What is the highest mountain range in South America?

MISSING LETTER PROVERB

Fill in each missing letter, indicated by an X, to make a well-known proverb.

TXX MOXE TXX MEXXIEX

WORD POWER **Architecture & Construction**

They say a good vocabulary is the foundation of learning.
Master these terms related to architecture and construction
and you will build yourself a fine edifice.

. . . .

1. **raze** ('rayz) *v.*—A: build up.
B: dig a foundation. C: tear down.

2. **dexterous** ('dek-ster-us) *adj.*—
A: skillful. B: left-handed. C: turned
clockwise.

3. **jury-rig** ('jur-ee-rig) *v.*—A: set up
permanently. B: construct in a
makeshift fashion. C: glaze.

4. **stud** ('stuhd) *n.*—A: slang for
a good carpenter. B: leveling bar.
C: upright post.

5. **on spec** (on 'spek) *adv.*—
A: using blueprints. B: without a
contract. C: ahead of schedule.

6. **garret** ('gar-it) *n.*—A: attic room.
B: pantry or extra kitchen room.
C: basement room.

7. **annex** ('a-neks) *n.*—
A: supplementary structure.
B: underground dwelling.
C: foundation.

8. **wainscot** ('wayn-skoht) *n.*—
A: intricate plasterwork.
B: scaffolding. C: paneled part of a
wall.

9. **rotunda** (roh-'tun-duh) *n.*—
A: central column. B: circular
room. C: revolving door.

10. **plumb** ('plum) *adj.*—A: not
linked, as pipes. B: past its prime.
C: vertical.

11. **aviary** ('ay-vee-ehr-ee) *n.*—
A: house for birds. B: airport
terminal. C: open lobby.

12. **corrugated** ('kor-eh-gayt-ed)
adj.—A: with closed doors.
B: rusted. C: having a wavy
surface.

13. **mezzanine** ('meh-zeh-neen)
n.—A: lowest balcony floor.
B: domed ceiling. C: marble
counter.

14. **cornice** ('kor-nes) *n.*—
A: meeting of two walls.
B: decorative top edge.
C: steeple or spire.

15. **vestibule** ('ves-teh-buyl) *n.*—
A: dressing room. B: lobby.
C: staircase.

Fall Traditions

ACROSS

1. Overnight lodging
6. Owns
9. Exclamation of discovery
12. Visitor to Wonderland
13. Boxing great Muhammad
14. Female
15. Inventor Nikola
16. Fall brings the ___ moon
18. Locations
20. ___ the Wild
21. ___ autumn leaves
24. Detests
25. State firmly
26. Unusual
29. Witch
30. Try to prevent
31. Baking an apple ___
34. Bullet point
35. Exclamation of distress (2 words)
36. Graded
40. Decorating with ___ corn
42. Long-legged wading bird
43. Curriculum ___
45. Visiting the ___ patch
47. Sacred song or poem
51. Compass abbreviation
52. Large deer
53. ___ Lauder cosmetics
54. Scarlet
55. No's opposite
56. Beauty parlor

DOWN

1. Yoga need
2. Shout heard in the bull ring
3. ___ the season
4. Cream-filled pastry
5. Gain knowledge
6. Laughter syllables
7. Unfortunately
8. Mister
9. Secret or double
10. Urgency
11. Women's voices
17. By way of
19. Great white bird
21. Cheer word
22. Actress Gardner
23. Small barrel
24. "She's a woman of ___ word"
27. Devoured
28. Pay
30. Accomplished
31. 21st letter of the Greek alphabet
32. "That's it ___ nutshell" (2 words)
33. Extremely long time
35. City in Ukraine
36. More ready for picking
37. Mistreat
38. Recorded the speed
39. Sixth sense (abbrev.)
41. Backs of necks
43. Disgusting
44. Signs with a pen
46. Code
48. Airport code for Hartsfield-Jackson
49. Zodiac sign
50. Fellas

MIND MAZE # Loop the Loops

Each of these puzzles can be arranged so that one color forms an uninterrupted loop running through all four squares. Can you find it? You may rotate each square about its center but may not move it otherwise.

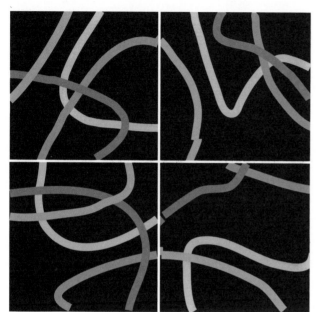

◄ 1

What tree gives
us prunes?

_____

2 ▶

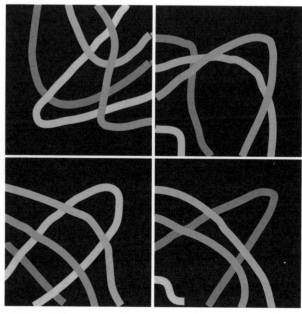

trivia

- Who played Batman in the 1997 movie *Batman & Robin*?

_____

Answers *(Do You Know? and Trivia answers are on page 224)*

PAGE 8

Fruit Punch

S	P	I	T		D	O	L	T	S		R	O	M	P
A	I	D	A		I	N	U	R	E		E	R	I	E
N	E	E	D		F	E	L	O	N		P	A	L	E
G	R	A	P	E	F	R	U	I	T		A	N	O	N
			O	D	E	S			I	D	I	G		
A	M	B	L	E	R		H	U	N	D	R	E	D	S
V	A	L	E	N		B	O	N	E	S		B	I	P
A	N	A	S		S	E	P	A	L		C	O	C	O
I	I	C		A	C	R	E	S		H	O	W	T	O
L	A	K	E	L	A	N	D		C	O	L	L	A	R
		B	A	E	R			C	O	L	D			
A	L	E	G		C	H	E	R	R	Y	P	I	C	K
G	I	R	L		E	A	G	E	R		L	O	R	I
E	T	R	E		L	L	A	M	A		A	W	O	L
D	A	Y	S		Y	O	D	E	L		Y	A	W	N

PAGE 9

Cage the Animals

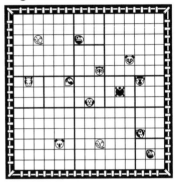

BLOCK ANAGRAM • MOUNTAIN CLIMBING

PAGE 10

Hourglass

(1) HAMSTER
(2) HAREMS
(3) SHAME
(4) SAME
(5) SEMI
(6) SMILE
(7) SIMPLE
(8) IMPULSE

PAGE 11

ABBA Hits

M	I	L	L		S	C	O	R	E		C	H	U	M
E	L	I	A		T	A	L	O	N		O	O	N	A
O	I	N	K		E	R	I	K	A		S	N	I	T
W	A	T	E	R	L	O	O		M	O	T	E	T	S
			L	U	L	L		T	O	D	A	Y		
H	A	V	A	N	A		H	A	R	D	S	H	I	P
O	Z	O	N	E		D	O	M	E	S		O	N	E
S	T	U	D		B	I	P	E	D		A	N	T	E
N	E	L		L	I	N	E	R		K	N	E	E	L
I	C	E	B	E	R	G	S		S	A	T	Y	R	S
		Z	E	S	T	Y		A	C	H	E			
L	A	V	I	S	H		F	E	R	N	A	N	D	O
E	B	O	N		D	O	U	S	E		T	E	R	N
S	L	U	G		A	R	R	O	W		E	R	I	C
T	E	S	S		Y	E	L	P	S		R	O	P	E

PAGE 12

Verbs

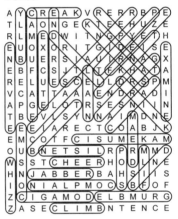

A verb, together with its subject and possibly a direct object, forms the basis of a sentence.

PAGE 13

Keep Going

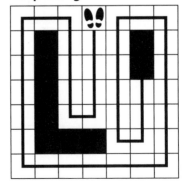

CHANGE ONE • SLUSH FUND

PAGE 14

Popular Pets

C	O	M	P		S	T	O	P	S		L	A	M	A
A	M	A	R		E	A	D	I	E		I	G	O	R
S	A	T	O		S	P	I	C	A		C	R	O	P
T	H	E	C	A	T	I	N	T	H	E	H	A	T	
E	A	R	L	I	E	R			O	W	E			
			A	N	T		S	E	R	E	N	A	D	E
O	R	B	I	T		C	L	A	S	S		R	A	T
L	O	A	M		C	E	A	S	E		S	I	L	O
A	A	R		S	A	D	I	E		S	W	A	I	N
F	R	I	G	H	T	E	N		B	E	I			
		H	A	H			G	R	A	N	D	E	E	
	A	D	O	G	O	F	F	L	A	N	D	E	R	S
E	R	O	S		L	I	L	A	C		L	E	N	T
D	A	R	T		I	S	E	R	E		E	R	S	E
E	L	K	S		C	H	E	E	R		R	E	T	E

PAGE 15

Escape Plan

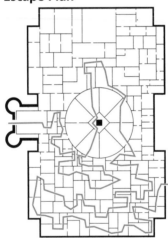

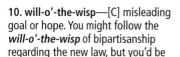

PAGE 16

Sport Maze

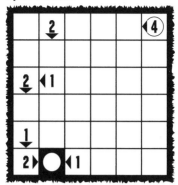

UNCANNY TURN • IS ABC

PAGE 17

Word Sudoku

R	A	Q	T	N	I	E	O	S
O	E	N	S	R	Q	T	A	I
I	T	S	E	O	A	N	Q	R
Q	O	R	I	A	E	S	T	N
T	N	I	R	S	O	Q	E	A
A	S	E	N	Q	T	I	R	O
N	Q	T	O	I	R	A	S	E
E	I	O	A	T	S	R	N	Q
S	R	A	Q	E	N	O	I	T

LETTERBLOCKS • ANATOMY / HABITAT

PAGE 18

Spot the Differences

PAGE 19

Checkmate!

M	E	O	W		A	B	B	E	S		A	Q	U	A
A	L	L	I		B	R	U	S	H		N	U	L	L
R	O	A	N		B	I	R	C	H		G	E	N	E
K	I	N	G	C	O	B	R	A		F	L	E	A	S
		N	O	T	E		P	E	R	O	N			
R	E	C	U	R	S		C	A	R	E	S	S	E	D
E	N	A	T	E		B	A	D	G	E		L	E	E
T	E	S	S		M	I	R	E	S		P	A	R	K
A	R	T		B	U	S	T	S		J	A	N	I	E
G	O	L	I	A	T	H	S		F	O	L	D	E	D
		E	R	A	T	O		T	U	B	A			
A	P	R	I	L		P	A	W	N	S	T	A	R	S
B	O	O	T		D	R	U	I	D		I	K	E	A
L	O	C	I		T	I	T	L	E		N	I	P	S
E	L	K	S		S	C	O	L	D		E	N	O	S

PAGE 20

Alice in Wonderland

1. hookah—[C] smoking pipe. Gerry found a shop downtown that offers supplies for his antique *hookah*.

2. platitudes—[A] trite sayings. Our coach offered a dozen peppy *platitudes* like "No pain, no gain."

3. welter—[A] toss among waves. Heading for shore, Karyn stayed focused on the buoy *weltering* in the distance.

4. lory—[B] type of parrot. Mitch set off for Australia to study and photograph the *lory* in the wild.

5. impertinent—[C] rude. "Would it be too *impertinent* to point out that I can hear you snoring six rows back?"

6. languid—[B] sluggish or weak. By three in the afternoon, I am too *languid* to think about anything but coffee and a couch.

7. ungainly—[B] clumsy or awkward. Is it me, or is he the most *ungainly* mime you've ever seen?

8. livery—[B] uniform. The butler's rumpled *livery* made him a prime suspect in the disappearance of our dinner host.

9. antipathies—[C] feelings of dislike. I'd say there were some mild antipathies between the two speakers at the city hall meeting.

10. will-o'-the-wisp—[C] misleading goal or hope. You might follow the *will-o'-the-wisp* of bipartisanship regarding the new law, but you'd be foolish.

11. sally—[C] witty remark. Aside from the occasional *sally*, the sportscasters had little to offer.

12. griffin—[A] monster with wings. Felix was fascinated by the illustrations of the *griffin* in his mythology book.

13. cravat—[B] scarf-like necktie. I'm going to the party as James Bond—would he wear a *cravat*?

14. hansom—[A] horse-drawn carriage. The producer of Cinderella was troubled by the plan to transform the *hansom* into a pumpkin onstage.

15. sagaciously—[A] wisely. The critic *sagaciously* pointed out the logic holes in Tara's dense first novel.

VOCABULARY RATINGS
9 and below: In a hole
10–12: Quick witted
13–15: Wonderful

PAGE 21

Sudoku

8	3	1	6	7	5	4	9	2
9	4	7	8	2	3	1	6	5
6	2	5	1	4	9	3	7	8
3	6	8	2	1	4	9	5	7
1	7	9	5	3	8	6	2	4
4	5	2	9	6	7	8	3	1
2	1	4	7	9	6	5	8	3
7	8	6	3	5	1	2	4	9
5	9	3	4	8	2	7	1	6

ONE LETTER LESS OR MORE • CABARET

Answers

PAGE 22

The Midas Touch

T	H	A	W		P	L	A	C	E		D	O	M	E
R	O	N	A		R	O	B	O	T		A	L	E	G
A	N	O	N		U	R	I	A	H		N	I	N	O
G	O	L	D	E	N	D	E	L	I	C	I	O	U	S
G	R	E	E	C	E				O	L	E			
			R	O	D		P	O	P	U	L	A	T	E
A	N	G	E	L		A	L	A	I			B	O	Y
G	O	L	D	E	N	P	A	R	A	C	H	U	T	E
E	R	I		I	S	I	S			H	A	T	E	D
E	M	B	R	A	C	E	D		R	I	P			
			E	L	K			A	L	P	A	C	A	
G	O	L	D	E	N	R	E	T	R	I	E	V	E	R
E	P	E	E		A	E	R	I	E		N	E	L	L
N	I	N	E		M	A	B	E	L		E	R	I	E
T	E	A	M		E	M	E	R	Y		D	Y	A	N

PAGE 23

Ring the Changes

1. Summer
2. Password
3. Overheat
4. Weightless

PAGE 24

Horoscope

UNCANNY TURN • CONFITURE

PAGE 25

Antiquity

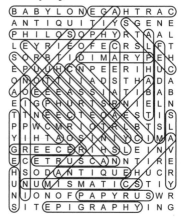

Antiquity generally refers to the period that begins with the introduction of writing.

PAGE 26

Hello Spring

PAGE 27

Sunny

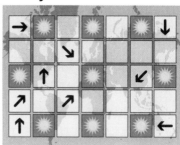

BLOCK ANAGRAM • COLLEGE TUITION

PAGE 28

Jump to It

69. Add 1 to the previous number, reverse the digits and add 1 more.

DOODLE PUZZLE • DiscOverIng

PAGE 29

Daddy Ditties

E	G	Y	P	T		R	O	T	C		A	N	T	A
L	A	U	R	A		O	P	A	H		S	C	A	D
M	R	M	O	M		T	E	R	I		L	A	L	A
	P	A	P	A	D	O	N	T	P	R	E	A	C	H
			E	L	I				M	O	E			
A	L	F	R	E	D	O		B	U	M	P	K	I	N
G	O	A	T	S		A	T	O	N	E		A	S	O
N	A	R	Y		S	T	A	L	K		D	Y	E	S
E	T	C		N	E	H	R	U		D	E	A	R	E
W	H	E	R	E	A	S		S	H	O	C	K	E	D
			E	L	S			A	N	I				
P	A	P	A	L	O	V	E	S	M	A	M	B	O	
E	G	A	D		N	A	N	A		T	A	R	O	T
N	E	N	E		A	S	I	N		E	T	A	P	E
N	E	E	R		L	E	D	A		D	E	N	S	E

PAGE 30

The Planet Suite

1. Pluto
2. Neptune
3. 1969
4. The solar system
5. Saturn
6. Mars
7. Venus
8. Earth
9. Meteorites
10. Mercury
11. Metropolis
12. Uranus
13. Gustav Holst
14. Tim Burton
15. Saturn
16. Primarily ice
17. Saturn
18. Neil Armstrong

PAGE 31

Sudoku Twin

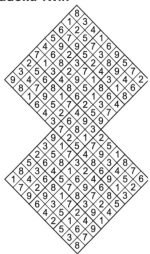

DOUBLETALK • BROACH/BROOCH

PAGE 32

Word Pyramid

C

(1) AC

(2) ARC

(3) ORCA

(4) ROACH

(5) CHORAL

(6) CHOLERA

(7) BACHELOR

PAGE 33

Play Ball

PAGE 34

Keep Going

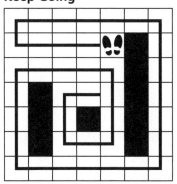

CHANGE ONE • DROP OUT

PAGE 35

Space Travel

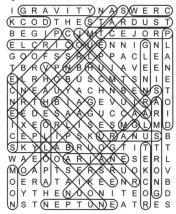

In the beginning of space travel Russia achieved successes, but it was later overtaken by the United States.

PAGE 36

Sky Sights

PAGE 37

Snow

Group 4. The crystals always link up a short and a long arm. In group 4 they link up two long arms.

REPOSITION PREPOSITION • WITH RESPECT TO

PAGE 38

Word Sudoku

T	F	V	R	U	O	N	A	L
O	A	N	F	V	L	T	R	U
U	L	R	N	T	A	F	O	V
V	N	O	A	R	F	L	U	T
L	R	T	V	N	U	A	F	O
F	U	A	L	O	T	V	N	R
A	T	L	O	F	R	U	V	N
R	V	U	T	A	N	O	L	F
N	O	F	U	L	V	R	T	A

LETTERBLOCKS • LEGGINGS / SANDALS

PAGE 39

Disaster Flicks

D	E	N	Y		O	R	A	L			S	E	R	A
A	L	E	E		N	O	N	E	T		H	A	I	L
C	O	A	L		H	A	N	O	I		O	R	C	A
A	I	R	P	L	A	N	E		T	E	E	T	E	R
			I	N	S		H	A	R	S	H			
E	C	H	O	E	D		S	A	N	S		Q	U	O
D	R	I	P	S		S	A	D	I	E		U	R	N
N	A	N	A		I	O	N	I	C		C	A	G	E
A	N	D		E	N	D	E	D		L	A	K	E	R
S	E	E		A	F	A	R		C	A	R	E	S	S
			N	O	S	E	S		H	A	T			
A	M	B	L	E	R		P	O	S	E	I	D	O	N
L	A	U	D		N	U	R	S	E		R	I	L	E
I	N	R	E		O	M	A	N	I		I	V	A	N
S	I	G	N		A	M	I	N		S	A	F	E	

PAGE 40

Sport Maze

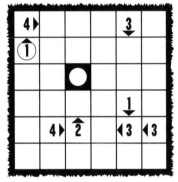

UNCANNY TURN •
HAD NO SOLE

PAGE 41

Futoshiki

3	1	2	4	5
5	3 < 4	2	1
1 < 2	5	3	4
4	5	3	1 < 2
2	4 > 1	5 > 3

CONNECT TWO •
BONELESS____RIBS
ALL_____ALONE
LONG _____SHORT
FIRM_____ESTIMATE

PAGE 42

Movies

B	A	L	I		M	O	L	A	R		D	O	U	R
A	M	I	D		O	P	I	N	E		E	D	G	E
L	O	N	E		R	A	N	D	I		T	O	L	D
M	I	D	N	I	G	H	T	I	N	P	A	R	I	S
			T	R	A				D	O	I			
L	U	C	I	A	N	O		F	E	L	L	O	W	S
O	R	A	T	E		D	A	L	E	Y		B	A	A
G	A	R	Y		R	E	C	U	R		W	E	L	T
I	N	O		L	E	T	T	S		G	I	L	D	A
C	O	M	P	A	S	S		H	E	L	L	I	O	N
			U	Z	I				D	A	D			
C	R	A	Z	Y	S	T	U	P	I	D	L	O	V	E
L	O	D	Z		T	U	N	I	C		I	D	O	L
A	N	I	L		E	N	A	C	T		F	E	L	L
P	A	T	E		D	E	S	K	S		E	A	S	E

PAGE 43

Train Your Brain

Cool Eggs

 B. At each stage the small blue and pink circles in the eclipse change places. The larger blue circle moves one place to the right at each stage, so it ends up to the right of the eclipse.

Designer Flag

 D. The black dot moves one side clockwise at each stage and alternates outside and inside the rectangle. The star moves in exactly the same way. The eclipse alternates between two sides, first inside, then outside the rectangle.

PAGE 44

Snakeskin

1. The skin's color pattern consists of black alternated with a colored square. The piece of snakeskin on a yellow background gets the same color as the background.

DOODLE PUZZLE • ReadY

PAGE 45

Sudoku

1	2	5	3	8	7	4	6	9
6	3	4	1	9	5	2	8	7
8	9	7	4	2	6	1	5	3
5	7	6	8	3	4	9	1	2
9	4	8	2	6	1	3	7	5
2	1	3	7	5	9	6	4	8
4	6	2	5	7	3	8	9	1
3	5	9	6	1	8	7	2	4
7	8	1	9	4	2	5	3	6

ONE LETTER LESS OR MORE •
SURGEON

PAGE 46

Trivial Pursuit 1938

1. Kal-El, Krypton
2. Clark Kent
3. Jonathan and Martha Kent, Smallville, KS
4. Metropolis, the Daily Planet
5. Bud Collyer
6. Lois Lane
7. Perry White, Jimmy Olsen
8. Green Kryptonite
9. George Reeves
10. Christopher Reeve
11 John Williams
12. Jerry Siegel and Joe Shuste

PAGE 47
Temperature Extremes

B	O	W	S		S	O	L	T	I		M	O	N	O
A	C	H	E		U	T	A	H	N		A	P	A	R
C	H	I	C		P	O	S	E	D		L	A	L	A
H	O	T	L	I	P	S	H	O	U	L	I	H	A	N
		U	R	E				S	A	C				
S	P	I	D	E	R	S		A	T	T	E	M	P	T
N	I	N	E	S		T	E	R	R	E		A	R	E
A	C	E	D		F	O	G	G	Y		B	O	O	R
F	O	P		B	O	N	G	O		F	U	R	O	R
U	T	T	E	R	L	Y		N	U	L	L	I	F	Y
			D	A	L			N	I	L				
C	O	L	D	C	O	M	F	O	R	T	F	A	R	M
A	L	A	I		W	A	L	D	O		R	U	E	D
S	I	N	E		E	M	A	I	L		O	R	E	S
H	O	E	D		R	E	P	E	L		G	A	L	E

PAGES 48
Treasure Island Express

If you've followed the clues correctly you should have destroyed the track as shown in red, in the order 1–7 (did you realize that a "giant scull" is the oar, and not the giant skull?). This leaves the brown route shown as the only possible route to the treasure, marking the X circled in the top right-hand corner as the spot.

PAGE 49
Garden Variety

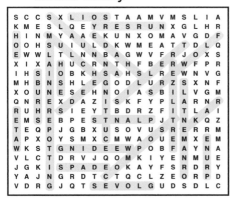

```
S C C S X L I O S T A A M V M S L I A
K M E S L Q E Y R E S R U N X G L H R
H I N M Y A A E K U N X O M A V G D F
O O H S U I U L D K W M E A T T D L Q
E W W L T L N N B A G W V F R J O X S
X I X A H U C R N T H F B E R W F P R
I H S I O B K H S A H S L R E W N V G
M H B N S H L E G O D L U R Z S X N F
X O U N E S E H N O I A S B I L V G M
Q N R E X D A Z I S K F Y P L A R N R
R U H R S I E Y T B D R Z F I T L A I
E M S E B P E S T N A L P J T N K Q Z
T E Q P J G B X U S O V U S R E R R M
A P X O Y S M X C M W A O U E M X E M
W K S T G N I D E E W P O B F A Y N A
V L C T D R V J Q O M K I Y E N M U E
J G K I S P A D E O K A Y F S R D R Y
Y A J N G R D T C T Q C L Z E O R P D
V D R G J Q T S E V O L G U D S D L C
```

PAGE 50
1950s No. 1 Hits

M	E	N	U		B	A	L	L	S		I	B	A	R
I	V	A	N		E	L	I	O	T		M	Y	T	H
M	A	Y	B	E	L	L	E	N	E		P	E	L	E
I	N	S	I	S	T	E	D		A	R	A	B	I	A
			A	T	E	N		E	M	E	R	Y		
H	I	S	S	E	D		F	R	I	T	T	E	R	S
A	N	T	E	S		C	L	I	N	E		L	I	T
S	C	A	D		S	L	A	N	G		V	O	L	E
T	A	G		T	H	A	T	S		C	O	V	E	N
A	N	G	R	I	E	S	T		T	O	L	E	D	O
			E	A	R	L	S		R	O	T	C		
F	E	R	R	E	T		C	A	P	T	A	I	N	S
I	L	L	E		E	A	R	T	H	A	N	G	E	L
G	A	E	L		R	A	I	S	A		I	O	N	E
S	L	E	Y		S	A	B	O	T		C	R	E	W

PAGE 51
Cage the Animals

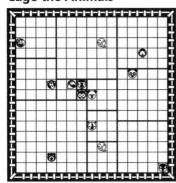

BLOCK ANAGRAM •
ENGAGEMENT

PAGE 52
Hourglass

(1) FEDERAL
(2) FEARED
(3) FADER
(4) DEAF
(5) FEUD
(6) FREUD
(7) REFUND
(8) FOUNDER

PAGE 53
Punny and Funny 1

S	O	S	O		D	R	A	M	A		E	A	C	H
A	M	O	R		R	E	B	U	T		A	G	H	A
R	E	N	D		E	N	A	C	T		G	R	I	N
A	G	A	I	N	S	T	T	H	E	C	L	O	C	K
H	A	R	N	E	S	S			M	O	E			
			A	N	Y		D	E	P	O	S	I	T	S
G	L	A	R	E		T	R	I	T	T		C	O	P
R	O	L	Y		V	E	I	N	S		V	E	R	A
A	G	O		F	I	L	L	E		C	I	D	E	R
M	Y	T	H	I	C	A	L		H	A	S			
			O	A	T		N	O	T	I	C	E	S	
P	O	I	N	T	O	F	N	O	R	E	T	U	R	N
E	A	V	E		R	E	E	L	S		I	R	A	E
A	H	A	S		I	R	A	T	E		N	I	T	A
R	U	N	T		A	N	T	E	S		G	O	O	D

PAGE 54
Binairo

I	O	I	I	O	O	I	O	I	O	O	I
O	I	O	I	O	I	O	I	I	O	I	O
O	O	I	O	I	O	I	I	O	I	O	I
I	I	O	O	I	O	I	O	O	I	I	O
O	O	I	I	O	I	O	O	I	O	I	I
I	I	O	O	I	O	O	I	I	O	O	I
I	I	O	I	O	I	I	O	O	I	O	O
O	O	I	I	O	O	I	O	I	O	I	I
I	I	O	O	I	I	O	I	O	I	O	O
I	O	O	I	I	O	O	I	O	I	I	O
O	O	I	O	O	I	I	O	I	O	I	I
O	I	I	O	I	I	O	I	O	I	O	O

SANDWICH • GUARD

Answers

PAGE 55

Row Your Boat

5 people. Four oarsmen and a coxswain. You can discover this because there is not an extra oar visible at the front of the top image.

DOODLE PUZZLE • FeedBack

PAGE 56

On the Increase

A	R	I	D		S	A	R	O	D		B	R	I	O
D	E	M	I		A	B	O	V	E		L	O	C	K
O	M	A	N		B	E	D	I	M		I	T	E	A
B	I	G	G	I	R	L	S	D	O	N	T	C	R	Y
E	X	E	D	R	A			L	A	H				
		O	A	S	T		M	I	N	E	R	A	L	
A	M	E	N	T		U	S	E	S			A	A	A
B	I	G	G	E	R	F	I	S	H	T	O	F	R	Y
L	E	A		E	T	N	A		S	A	I	L		
E	N	D	R	U	N	S		S	A	I	L			
		E	R	E			T	A	C	O	M	A		
T	H	E	B	I	G	G	E	S	T	L	O	S	E	R
R	O	T	O		A	R	E	T	E		L	A	D	I
A	M	O	R		D	O	L	E	S		O	G	E	E
P	E	N	N		E	G	Y	P	T		R	E	A	L

PAGE 57

Keep Going

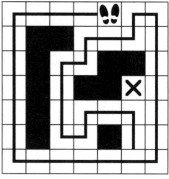

DELETE ONE • DELETE S AND FIND PALMISTRY.

PAGE 58

Sunny

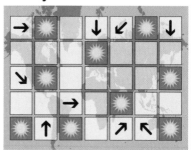

BLOCK ANAGRAM • HURRICANE

PAGE 59

Pretty Beat-Up

H	E	M	P		F	L	A	T	T		R	A	T	E
E	V	E	R		R	A	R	E	E		U	S	E	R
R	I	S	E		E	D	I	N	A		S	E	E	N
B	L	A	C	K	E	Y	E	D	S	U	S	A	N	S
			L	I	Z			P	R	O				
S	A	L	U	T	E		A	N	O	N		S	A	M
A	B	O	D	E		O	M	O	O		W	A	V	E
B	L	U	E	R	I	B	B	O	N	P	A	N	E	L
R	E	P	S		M	I	L	K		A	N	D	R	E
E	R	E		C	I	T	E		I	G	N	I	T	E
		A	C	T			N	E	A					
A	L	L	B	L	A	C	K	A	N	D	B	L	U	E
N	O	A	H		T	A	L	I	A		E	A	R	L
E	R	N	O		O	V	E	R	T		E	R	A	S
W	E	A	R		R	E	E	S	E		S	A	L	E

PAGE 60

Actresses

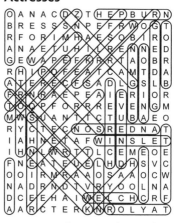

An actress performs in a theatrical performance or in a film, on TV or as a cartoon character.

PAGE 61

Sport Maze

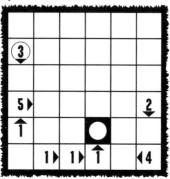

UNCANNY TURN • POETRY

PAGE 62

Tee for Two

T	I	F	F		S	H	A	P	E		U	T	E	S
A	L	O	U		H	E	L	I	X		N	U	D	E
R	I	A	L		E	L	E	C	T		E	M	I	L
T	A	L	L	T	A	L	E		E	N	A	M	E	L
			P	E	T			R	O	S	Y			
A	T	T	A	C	H	E		T	I	N	Y	T	O	T
D	O	U	G	H		A	C	H	O	O		U	W	E
M	O	R	E		B	R	I	A	R		U	C	L	A
I	N	K		M	U	L	A	N		A	S	K	E	R
T	E	E	T	I	M	E		A	M	N	E	S	T	Y
		Y	A	K	S			A	I	D				
A	N	T	L	E	R		T	U	R	N	T	A	I	L
D	I	R	E		U	L	E	N	T		O	L	G	A
A	N	O	N		S	E	E	D	Y		B	O	O	N
M	A	T	T		H	O	N	O	R		E	T	T	A

PAGE 63

A Round of Golf

1. The 19th hole
2. One under par
3. Ground under repair
4. Fairway
5. Sand trap
6. The golfer has an acquired problem of tremors, freezing, or jerking while putting
7. St. Andrews
8. Match play
9. Caddy
10. Ace
11. Air Shot or Whiff
12. A snowman - so called becasue an eight (8) looks similar to the body of a snowman.

PAGE 64

Hamilton Lingo

1. manumission—[B] the act of freeing from slavery. Alexander Hamilton: "[We are] a bunch of revolutionary *manumission* abolitionists."

2. complicit—[C] associating with or participating in. Thomas Jefferson: "I am *complicit* in watchin' him grabbin' at power and kiss it."

3. equivocate—[A] waffle. Hamilton: "I will not *equivocate* on my opinion."

4. enterprising—[A] go-getting. Jefferson: "These are wise words, *enterprising* men quote 'em."

5. homilies—[B] sermons. Aaron Burr: "These are things that the *homilies* and hymns won't teach ya."

6. venerated—[B] honored. George Washington: "I'm ... the *venerated* Virginian veteran."

7. restitution—[C] amends. Burr: "He woulda been dead or destitute without a cent or *restitution*."

8. dissidents—[A] dissenters. Jefferson: "If Washington isn't gon' listen to disciplined *dissidents* ..."

9. obfuscates—[C] confuses. James Madison: "Ask him a question: It glances off, he *obfuscates*, he dances."

10. jettison—[C] throw away. Hamilton: "There isn't a plan he doesn't *jettison*."

11. intemperate—[C] unrestrained. Burr: "*Intemperate* indeed, good man."

12. vacuous—[A] empty or blank. Jefferson: "Gimme some dirt on this *vacuous* mass so we can at last unmask him."

13. intransigent—[A] stubborn. Hamilton: "These Virginians are ... being *intransigent*."

14. inimitable—[A] incomparable or unrivaled. Burr: "I am *inimitable*. I am an original."

15. disparage—[B] speak ill of. Philip Hamilton: "He *disparaged* my family's legacy in front of a crowd."

VOCABULARY RATINGS
9 and below: Chorus
10–12: Headline
13–15: Tony Winner

PAGE 65

Recycler

Logo C. Logo A and D are reversed, B colors are changed, E and F are warped.

DOODLE PUZZLE • SunSpots

PAGE 66

Spot the Differences

PAGE 67

Sudoku X

3	7	9	1	4	6	8	5	2
5	4	6	2	9	8	1	7	3
8	1	2	7	3	5	9	4	6
1	8	7	9	5	3	2	6	4
2	3	4	6	8	1	5	9	7
9	6	5	4	2	7	3	8	1
4	2	1	5	7	9	6	3	8
7	5	3	8	6	2	4	1	9
6	9	8	3	1	4	7	2	5

LETTER LINE • PILGRIMAGE; GLEAM, REGAL, MAGPIE, IMPERIL

PAGE 68

High

PAGE 69

Horoscope

UNCANNY TURN • SLITHERED

PAGE 70

Kakuro

1	3	6		3	2	4
5	6		5	9	4	
2	1	6		2		
		9	2	8	3	
6		8	6		5	
9	4	5		3	1	2
7	2			4	9	1

MISSING LETTER PROVERB • ALL GOOD THINGS MUST COME TO AN END.

PAGE 71

Low

B	R	A	C		S	E	R	I	F		O	I	L	S
L	O	B	O		E	R	I	C	A		K	N	E	E
O	M	E	N		R	E	G	A	L		S	T	I	R
C	A	T	T	L	E	C	A	L	L		A	H	A	B
			R	U	N	T			I	O	N	E		
E	F	F	A	C	E		L	A	B	R	A	D	O	R
S	L	A	C	K		R	A	L	L	Y		U	N	A
T	E	N	T		R	I	D	G	E		M	M	C	C
O	U	S		M	E	D	E	A		M	A	P	L	E
P	R	E	S	U	M	E	D		P	A	U	S	E	D
			T	I	M	E			E	A	R	N		
M	A	T	E		D	E	S	P	I	C	A	B	L	E
E	L	I	S		I	C	H	O	R		L	A	I	N
R	E	N	T		E	R	O	D	E		O	L	A	V
V	E	G	A		D	U	P	E	D		A	I	R	Y

PAGE 72

A Brush with Beauty

1. Water lilies
2. Sunflowers
3. Georgia O'Keeffe
4. Salvadore Dali
5. Bruegel the Elder
6. Hieronymus Bosch
7. Primavera
8. Titian
9. Andy Warhol
10. Pablo Picasso
11. Tahiti
12. Jackson Pollock
13. Still life
14. Girl with a Pearl Earring

PAGE 73

1960s Sitcoms

PAGE 74

Getting Shirty

Polo shirt 4. All the other polo shirts have pointed collars.

REPOSITION PREPOSITION • ACCORDING TO

PAGE 75

Fall Fun

PAGE 76

Opposites Attract

#1	#2
1. e	1. g
2. j	2. e
3. f	3. h
4. i	4. d
5. a	5. a
6. c	6. j
7. b	7. f
8. d	8. i
9. h	9. c
10. g	10. b

PAGE 77

Trivial Pursuit 1976

1. Gerald Ford
2. George Washington
3. Declaration of Independence
4. Replica of the Liberty Bell
5. $2 bill
6. Karl Wallenda
7. Johnny Cash
8. Bicentennial Minutes

TEST YOUR RECALL • MUHAMMAD ALI

PAGE 78

How Lovely!

A	G	A	R		S	H	A	D	Y		F	L	O	W
T	A	L	E		T	E	P	E	E		I	O	T	A
I	B	I	S		A	R	E	N	T		E	V	I	L
L	O	V	E	B	I	R	D		I	N	S	E	C	T
T	R	E	M	O	R					X				
				B	A	S	I	S		F	R	A	P	P	E
B	A	L	L	S		C	H	A	L	K		P	I	A
O	B	O	E		S	E	A	L	Y		S	L	U	R
S	U	V		C	A	R	L	A		L	O	E	S	S
S	T	E	R	E	O		L	I	L	A	C			
			M	A	D					E	V	A	D	E	D
P	L	A	T	E	S		L	O	V	E	L	I	F	E
O	A	T	H		I	R	E	N	E		L	O	F	T
O	N	C	E		D	E	V	I	L		E	D	I	E
L	A	H	R		E	D	I	T	S		D	E	E	R

PAGE 79

Home Port

A. Read as follows: the second and second last letter of the previous port are the first and last letter of the next port.

REPOSITION PREPOSITION • CONTRARY TO

PAGE 80

Mixed Vegetables

1. Bugs Bunny
2. Sir Walter Raleigh
3. Fine words
4 Cucumber
5. Turnips
6. Beets
7. Cabbage Patch Kids
8. Toy Story
9. Bean
10. Capsicum
11. Kava
12. A carrot
13. Eggplant
14. Durian
15. Zucchini
16. Lettuce

PAGE 81

Sudoku

3	7	2	1	8	6	5	9	4
4	5	8	3	9	7	6	2	1
6	9	1	2	4	5	3	8	7
2	4	5	8	6	1	7	3	9
9	8	6	7	3	4	1	5	2
7	1	3	5	2	9	8	4	6
1	3	9	6	5	2	4	7	8
5	2	7	4	1	8	9	6	3
8	6	4	9	7	3	2	1	5

ONE LETTER LESS OR MORE •
FISHING

PAGE 82

Keep Going

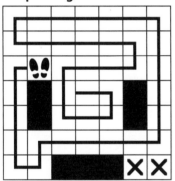

CHANGE ONE • DULL DOWN

PAGE 83

1970s No. 1 Hits

A	R	G	O		D	R	E	A	M		T	B	A	R
B	O	O	B		U	I	N	T	A		A	R	L	O
C	L	O	S	E	T	O	Y	O	U		S	O	L	O
S	E	N	O	R	I	T	A		N	I	T	W	I	T
			L	I	E	S		B	A	D	E	N		
A	L	I	E	N	S		C	O	L	O	S	S	A	L
B	E	L	T	S		H	O	B	O	S		U	V	A
O	G	L	E		M	A	M	B	A		A	G	E	D
D	A	B		C	A	S	E	Y		S	C	A	R	E
E	L	E	M	E	N	T	S		H	E	A	R	T	S
		T	E	D	D	Y		N	E	A	P			
M	A	H	L	E	R		P	O	R	T	U	G	A	L
E	R	E	I		I	T	S	T	O	O	L	A	T	E
T	E	R	N		L	O	I	R	E		C	L	E	M
A	S	E	A		L	O	S	E	S		O	L	E	A

PAGE 84

Futoshiki

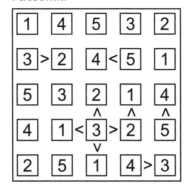

CONNECT TWO •
CALCULATED _ RISK
COUNTLESS __ NUMBERS
MUTE _____ SOUND
BIG _____ BABY

PAGE 85

Word Sudoku

A	W	I	T	R	D	E	M	L
M	L	R	E	I	W	A	D	T
E	D	T	M	A	L	W	R	I
T	E	W	I	D	R	M	L	A
L	R	D	A	M	T	I	W	E
I	A	M	W	L	E	R	T	D
R	M	L	D	E	A	T	I	W
D	T	A	R	W	I	L	E	M
W	I	E	L	T	M	D	A	R

LETTERBLOCKS • MANAGER /
PARTNER

PAGE 86

Twin Openers 1

PAGE 87

Alpinism

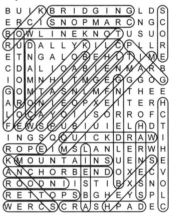

Buildering, usually illegal climbing
of the exterior of buildings, is a new,
exciting hype.

Answers

PAGE 88

Sudoku Twin

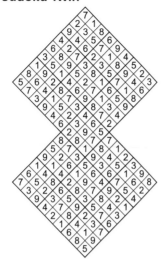

DOUBLETALK • THRONE / THROWN

PAGE 89

Sport Maze

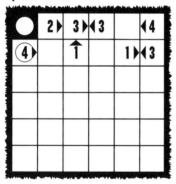

UNCANNY TURN • COUPLES

PAGE 90

Name That Dessert

TIRASUMI. The last syllable, SU, is always swapped with the successive syllables of the first word, so TI is swapped first, then RA and then MI.

TRANSADDITION • ADD I AND FIND "THE RAILROAD TRAIN".

PAGE 91

At the Lake

PAGES 92

Honeycomb Crossword

```
        D A Y D R E A M
      R Y           U A
      O   N E U R O N   R
      L   O       G E   G
      R M   M I C A   V   A
      E O   R O   M C   A   R
      V N   O     E D   E
    O R G A N Z A   C U R R A N T
      U A     I       R R S
      T   L N S   T E   D I
      G L   E T C H   N N
      O   O G     A U   O
        I   N O U G A T   D
      N A               C E
        G O L D R U S H
```

PAGE 93

Star-Crossed

B. The contents of each hexagon are determined by the contents of the two hexagons directly below it. Stars are only carried forward when they appear once in a position. When they appear twice in the same position, they are not carried forward.

PAGE 94

Masquerade

Color 5. Every fourth triangle is red.

DOODLE PUZZLE • UnderDog

PAGE 95

Twin Openers 2

PAGE 96

Trivial Pursuit 1948

1. Texas Star Theater
2. Kukla, Fran and Ollie
3. The Original Amateur Hour
4. Toast of the Town
5. Meet the Press
6. Candid Camera
7. Studio One
8. 7PM to 10PM Central Mountain

TEST YOUR RECALL • ALBERT ARNOLD GORE JR.

PAGE 97

Chairman of the Board

P	A	I	R		C	A	B	E	R		W	A	I	F
O	N	C	E		A	G	I	L	E		A	N	T	I
W	I	T	C	H	C	R	A	F	T		I	G	E	T
E	M	U	L	A	T	E	S		U	T	T	E	R	S
R	E	S	I	D	U	E		G	R	U	E	L		
			N	O	S		C	O	N	C	R	E	T	E
O	F	T	E	N		D	E	R	E	K		Y	E	N
L	A	H	R		C	O	D	E	D		F	E	N	D
O	V	A		R	O	W	A	N		L	A	S	T	S
R	E	T	A	I	L	E	R		D	A	D			
			S	T	O	O	L		L	O	V	E	S	T	O
P	I	L	O	T	S		M	A	N	E	A	T	E	R
O	L	I	N		S	U	M	M	E	R	W	I	N	D
S	A	F	E		A	N	D	I	E		A	N	T	E
E	Y	E	D		L	U	C	A	S		Y	G	O	R

210

PAGE 98

Literature

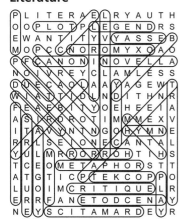

Literary authors want to convey a message with their texts in an artistic manner.

PAGE 99

Sudoku

4	7	9	8	1	3	5	6	2
3	5	6	9	4	2	8	7	1
2	8	1	7	6	5	4	9	3
6	9	3	2	5	1	7	4	8
1	4	8	3	7	9	2	5	6
5	2	7	6	8	4	1	3	9
8	3	4	1	9	7	6	2	5
9	1	5	4	2	6	3	8	7
7	6	2	5	3	8	9	1	4

ONE LETTER LESS OR MORE •
ROADBLOCK

PAGE 100

Famous Leos

PAGE 101

Pick a Side

Angle 5. We see the back of the castle. The small tower
on the left in front should be on the left in the back. The small tower on the right in back should be on the right in the front.

DOODLE PUZZLE • EinSTEIN

PAGE 102

Binairo

O	O	I	O	I	I	O	I	I	O	I
O	O	I	O	I	O	I	I	O	I	I
I	I	O	I	O	O	I	O	I	I	O
I	O	I	I	O	I	O	I	I	O	O
O	I	I	O	I	I	O	I	O	O	I
I	I	O	I	I	O	I	O	O	I	O
O	O	I	I	O	I	I	O	I	O	I
I	I	O	O	I	I	O	I	O	I	O
I	I	O	I	O	O	I	O	I	O	I
O	O	I	I	O	I	I	O	I	I	O
I	I	O	O	I	O	O	I	O	I	I

SANDWICH • HOUND

PAGE 103

Sport Maze

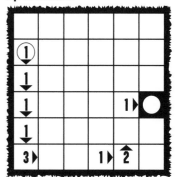

UNCANNY TURN • OR HUGE CATS

PAGE 104

Keep Going

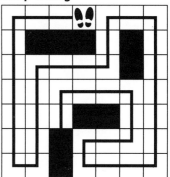

DELETE ONE • DELETE T AND FIND SINGAPORE

Answers

Word Sudoku

G	R	A	U	M	S	T	D	I
S	U	D	I	R	T	M	G	A
M	T	I	G	D	A	R	U	S
A	G	M	T	U	D	S	I	R
I	S	R	M	A	G	U	T	D
U	D	T	S	I	R	G	A	M
T	A	U	D	S	M	I	R	G
R	M	G	A	T	I	D	S	U
D	I	S	R	G	U	A	M	T

LETTERBLOCKS • BIOMASS / COMPOST

Fall Baking

F	I	G		V	E	N	I		A	N	T	S
O	N	A		I	R	I	S		G	O	A	T
O	R	R		C	R	A	N	B	E	R	R	Y
D	E	B	U	T		S	O	O	N			
			M	I	D		T	O	D	A	T	E
C	A	R	A	M	E	L		T	A	M	E	D
A	B	E			W	A	R			O	R	E
D	E	A	N	S		P	U	M	P	K	I	N
S	T	R	E	A	M		B	A	R			
		A	L	A	S		N	O	R	A	D	
B	U	T	T	E	R	N	U	T		E	N	E
A	S	H	E		C	A	S	E		A	T	L
T	E	E	N		O	P	A	L		P	I	E

Carnival

Vu. Read each word like three sequential letters from right to left.

REPOSITION PREPOSITION • WITH REFERENCE TO

Outlines

N. All letters that only appear once have a red outline.

DOODLE PUZZLE • ZeBra

Camping Out

H	I	K	E		F	L	A	B		A	K	A
O	D	I	N		A	E	R	O		R	A	D
P	A	P	A		C	A	M	P	F	I	R	E
		M	E	E	K		E	A	S	E	L	
F	O	R	E	S	T		S	E	R	E	N	E
A	D	U	L	T		P	I	P	E			
N	E	E		V	E	T			F	A	Y	
		C	A	I	N		A	D	O	B	E	
P	A	R	A	D	E		S	M	O	R	E	S
A	R	E	N	A		K	A	Y	E			
S	L	E	E	P	I	N	G		S	L	A	G
T	E	D		T	R	E	E		N	I	N	E
E	S	S		S	E	E	S		T	E	N	T

Word Sudoku

S	P	D	L	U	R	Y	I	E
I	U	E	S	Y	D	L	R	P
Y	L	R	I	P	E	D	S	U
E	R	U	P	L	S	I	D	Y
P	D	I	U	R	Y	E	L	S
L	S	Y	E	D	I	U	P	R
D	I	P	R	E	U	S	Y	L
U	Y	L	D	S	P	R	E	I
R	E	S	Y	I	L	P	U	D

LETTERBLOCKS • SKIMMER / SPATULA

Word Pyramid

E

(1) BE
(2) BEL
(3) ABLE
(4) TABLE
(5) STABLE
(6) BATTLES
(7) SEAT BELT

Sudoku

4	9	1	8	6	2	7	5	3
2	3	7	9	5	4	6	1	8
8	5	6	1	7	3	4	9	2
5	8	9	2	1	6	3	4	7
7	2	4	3	9	8	5	6	1
1	6	3	5	4	7	8	2	9
3	1	8	4	2	5	9	7	6
9	7	5	6	8	1	2	3	4
6	4	2	7	3	9	1	8	5

ONE LETTER LESS OR MORE • INTENSIVE

Themeless

I	D	E	S		S	T	U	P	A		I	R	K	S
C	E	L	T		H	A	N	O	I		D	E	N	T
H	E	L	I	C	O	P	T	E	R		I	D	E	A
O	R	A	T	O	R	I	O		P	R	O	P	E	R
R	E	S	C	U	E	R		G	L	A	C	E		
			H	R	S		P	L	A	T	Y	P	U	S
F	A	C	E	T		M	I	E	N	S		P	R	E
A	L	A	S		P	E	N	N	E		S	E	N	T
C	A	B		B	A	R	O	N		H	A	R	S	H
T	R	A	N	S	M	I	T		B	A	N			
		L	E	A	P	T		B	A	G	G	A	G	E
S	P	L	A	S	H		M	A	R	A	U	D	E	D
P	O	E	T		L	E	A	N	N	R	I	M	E	S
O	G	R	E		E	L	I	D	E		N	I	N	E
T	O	O	N		T	A	N	S	Y		E	T	A	L

Big Words 1

O	A	K	S		S	E	D	E	R		I	C	O	N
C	L	I	P		A	T	O	N	E		G	A	T	O
T	I	N	E		T	H	I	S	A		N	C	O	S
A	B	D	E	R	I	A	N		C	H	O	O	S	Y
D	I	S	C	E	R	N		S	T	E	R	E		
			H	O	E		S	T	I	L	E	T	T	O
V	I	B	E	S		S	T	R	O	P		H	I	P
E	N	O	S		S	P	A	I	N		K	E	N	T
I	S	M		U	H	U	R	A		L	I	S	T	S
L	O	B	S	T	E	R	S		F	A	N			
		I	N	E	P	T		B	R	I	D	G	E	S
B	A	N	I	S	H		Q	U	I	D	N	U	N	C
R	E	A	P		E	L	U	D	E		E	L	S	A
A	R	T	E		R	E	I	G	N		S	C	U	D
D	Y	E	S		D	O	Z	E	D		S	H	E	S

PAGE 115

Missing Corner

Cube 3. Look at the cubes in pairs (vertical pairs on left and right sides). On the edge and in the center of each side the colors are repeated in the same order. The same pattern is repeated on the top.

TRANSADDITION • ADD O AND FIND "THE RINGS OF SATURN"

PAGE 116

Sunny

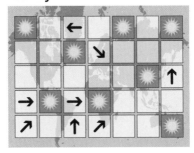

BLOCK ANAGRAM • NEBRASKA

PAGE 117

Eastwood Films

S	E	E	P		I	N	A	P	T		A	D	A	R
A	C	T	I		R	E	N	E	W		N	I	L	E
G	R	A	N	T	O	R	I	N	O		D	R	O	P
S	U	S	P	E	N	D	S		T	O	R	T	E	S
		O	N	E	S		M	I	L	E	Y			
A	C	H	I	E	R		S	O	M	E	W	H	A	T
G	R	A	N	T		S	I	R	E	N		A	V	E
A	I	N	T		S	I	D	E	D		B	R	A	E
M	E	G		D	O	L	L	S		S	E	R	I	N
A	D	E	Q	U	A	T	E		S	P	R	Y	L	Y
			M	U	M	P	S		S	A	R	A		
S	A	H	I	B	S		A	T	T	I	T	U	D	E
O	D	I	N		U	N	F	O	R	G	I	V	E	N
D	O	G	S		D	U	R	R	A		N	E	E	D
A	S	H	Y		S	T	O	M	P		G	A	P	S

PAGE 118

Number Cluster

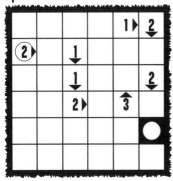

FRIENDS • EACH CAN HAVE THE PREFIX "SHIP" — TO FORM A NEW WORD.

PAGE 119

Spot the Differences

PAGE 120

Vegan Special

S	W	I	N	G		C	A	F	E		E	F	T	S
A	E	S	I	R		O	P	A	L		S	U	R	E
P	E	A	S	O	U	P	E	R	S		K	L	E	E
			O	S	E		M	A	R	I	L	Y	N	
A	L	C	O	V	E			E	M	O				
L	I	O	N	E	S	S		T	W	O	O	F	U	S
I	N	R	E	D		A	L	O	E	S		B	R	A
G	E	N	A		T	W	I	N	S		M	E	A	L
H	A	H		S	E	E	D	Y		L	I	A	N	A
T	R	U	S	T	E	D		S	T	E	R	N	U	M
		S	K	A			A	G	A	S	S	I		
B	I	K	I	N	I	S		T	R	I				
O	D	E	R		P	O	T	A	T	O	H	E	A	D
P	E	R	T		S	A	I	L		N	O	N	C	E
P	A	S	S		O	P	E	C		S	T	E	E	L

PAGE 121

Sport Maze

UNCANNY TURN • POSTMAN

PAGE 122

Environment

Governments and social organizations attempt to protect the environment.

PAGE 123

Famous Sagittarians

A	C	H	E		A	R	E	N	A		B	R	O	M
H	O	E	S		D	U	R	E	R		A	I	D	E
E	D	W	A	R	D	G	R	O	B	I	N	S	O	N
M	A	N	U	A	L			O	S	I	E	R	S	
			V	E	T		E	R	O	S				
T	B	I	L	I	S	I		N	E	P	H	E	W	S
H	O	S	E			M	A	C	A	O		V	I	I
E	R	S	K	I	N	E	C	A	L	D	W	E	L	L
T	E	E		N	O	S	E	S			A	R	C	O
A	R	I	A	D	N	E		E	M	B	R	Y	O	S
			D	I	E	S		D	U	E				
S	H	R	U	G	S			T	A	I	C	H	I	
T	O	U	L	O	U	S	E	L	A	U	T	R	E	C
O	B	I	T		C	H	E	A	T		C	E	R	E
P	O	N	S		H	E	N	C	E		H	E	E	D

Answers

PAGE 124

Sudoku X

2	5	9	4	1	8	7	6	3
8	3	6	7	5	2	4	9	1
1	4	7	6	3	9	5	2	8
9	2	3	5	7	4	1	8	6
6	7	4	1	8	3	2	5	9
5	1	8	2	9	6	3	4	7
4	8	1	3	6	5	9	7	2
3	6	2	9	4	7	8	1	5
7	9	5	8	2	1	6	3	4

LETTER LINE • UNIVERSITY;
VIRTUES, SURVEY, VEINS, TUNERS

PAGE 125

Sun, Moon, and Stars

1. **a.** Ra
2. **c.** Hair
3. **b.** Jabba the Hutt
4. **c.** 12
5. **a.** Argentina
6. **b.** Icarus
7. **a.** Somerset Maugham
8. **c.** The Who
9. **b.** The Unification Church
10. **a.** Judy Garland and James Mason

PAGE 126

Name That Beatles Tune!

Z	A	R	F		A	B	Y	S	M		A	S	A	P
E	C	H	O		M	A	O	R	I		N	O	N	O
S	T	I	R		P	A	N	I	C		A	M	O	K
T	U	N	N	E	L			H	E	L	E	N	E	
S	P	O	O	N	E	R		B	E	G	O	T		
		O	D	R	A		A	L	I	G	H	T	S	
I	S	B	N	S		P	U	R	L	S		I	R	E
D	O	L	E		M	I	L	N	E		S	N	I	T
E	R	A		P	I	N	T	O		M	A	G	M	A
S	E	C	T	I	L	E		W	R	E	N			
		K	O	O	K	S		L	E	T	I	T	B	E
A	L	B	A	N	Y			N	A	T	I	O	N	
L	E	I	S		W	O	M	A	N		A	N	N	E
T	A	R	T		A	R	O	S	E		T	E	E	M
O	D	D	S		Y	E	A	S	T		E	D	D	Y

PAGE 127

Keep Going

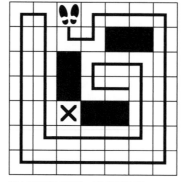

CHANGE ONE • TAKE BACK

PAGE 128

Kakuro

1	5	8		2	1	5	6
4	2			9	3		5	4
	4	7	1	8		4	9	7
8	3		1	6	8		
9	8	7	1		4	2	1
	8	2	5	7		5	8
2	6	9		8	9	1		3
1	4		3	1		2	8	9
5	7		8	2		7	9	6

MISSING LETTER PROVERB •
YOUTH IS WASTED ON THE YOUNG.

PAGE 129

Presidential Losers

H	E	R	B		C	R	O	P		S	A	G	E	S
E	L	I	A		O	I	S	E		I	S	E	R	E
A	L	F	L	A	N	D	O	N		S	T	R	I	A
P	E	E	L	I	N	G		D	E	T	R	A	C	T
			O	S	I	E	R		M	E	A	L		
C	A	J	O	L	E		E	V	E	R	Y	D	A	Y
A	L	O	N	E		S	P	I	E	S		F	R	O
R	A	H	S		S	K	I	E	R		S	O	A	K
L	M	N		S	P	I	N	S		S	E	R	G	E
S	O	M	E	T	I	M	E		M	A	N	D	E	L
		C	L	A	N		D	O	O	R	S			
L	O	C	A	T	E	D		P	R	A	I	R	I	E
I	R	A	T	E		A	A	R	O	N	B	U	R	R
A	R	I	E	L		T	E	A	S		L	I	E	N
M	A	N	D	Y		A	C	H	E		E	N	D	O

PAGE 130

Trivial Pursuit 1958

1. Mr. Potato Head
2. Play-Doh
5. Yahtzee
4. Hula Hoop
3. Silly Putty
6. Wiffle Ball
7. Colorforms

PAGE 131

Bicycle

Cycling is good for your health, pleasurable and in the city you often reach your destination faster than in a car.

PAGE 132–133

Circle of Color

Connect Six   **Relate Eight**

Five to Five

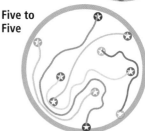

214

SANDWICH • AGE

Sudoku

4	5	9	7	3	8	2	1	6
6	8	2	5	4	1	7	3	9
3	7	1	9	6	2	8	5	4
2	1	5	8	7	4	6	9	3
8	9	6	1	2	3	4	7	5
7	3	4	6	5	9	1	8	2
5	2	3	4	1	7	9	6	8
9	6	7	2	8	5	3	4	1
1	4	8	3	9	6	5	2	7

ONE LETTER LESS OR MORE • AGREEMENT

Famous Arians

O	L	A	N		I	N	T	E	L		O	G	E	E
L	I	M	O		S	E	I	N	E		R	E	A	R
L	E	O	N	A	R	D	O	D	A	V	I	N	C	I
A	U	R	O	R	A			L	E	T	H	E		
			L	E	W		S	T	A	N				
R	A	V	I	O	L	I		P	O	S	T	M	E	N
O	M	I	T		T	R	I	N	I		O	L	A	
P	O	P	E	B	E	N	E	D	I	C	T	X	V	I
E	R	E		A	D	E	L	E		R	I	E	L	
S	T	R	A	N	D	S		R	A	P	I	E	R	S
		R	A	Y	S		S	R	O					
S	I	T	O	N				T	R	O	O	P	S	
T	H	O	M	A	S	J	E	F	F	E	R	S	O	N
L	A	M	A		A	A	R	A	U		A	S	E	A
O	D	E	S		G	N	A	R	L		L	A	M	P

Futoshiki

3	1	2	4	5
2	3 < 4	5	1
1 < 2	5	3	4
5 > 4 > 1	2	3
4	5	3	1 < 2

CONNECT TWO •
GLOBAL _____VILLAGE
ALMOST _____PREGNANT
FORGOTTEN __MEMORIES
LOUD _____WHISPER

Word Sudoku

LETTERBLOCKS • ORGANIC / RECYCLE

More Wordplay

U	P	O	N		P	U	P	I	L		A	J	A	R
S	A	L	A		A	T	O	N	E		C	O	C	O
S	T	E	R	N	R	E	P	R	O	A	C	H	E	S
R	E	G	R	E	S	S		I	N	T	E	N	S	E
		A	P	O				U	R	N				
T	A	R	T	A	N	S		W	R	I	T	E	R	S
O	R	I	E	L		C	U	R	I	A		V	I	C
T	E	N	D		P	A	L	E	S		R	I	V	E
E	N	S		G	E	N	U	S		P	E	C	A	N
M	A	E	W	E	S	T		T	H	I	S	T	L	E
		A	N	T				E	N	T				
S	T	O	R	I	E	S		M	A	U	R	I	C	E
C	O	M	M	E	R	C	I	A	L	P	A	P	E	R
O	N	I	T		E	A	R	L	E		I	S	N	T
W	I	T	H		D	R	E	A	D		N	O	T	E

Sunny

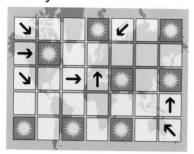

BLOCK ANAGRAM • CELEBRITIES

Curl It

On circle 12. All stones are located diametrically across from an opponent's stone.

TRANSADDITION • ADD S AND FIND "RAISES"

Trivial Pursuit 1956

1. Dino Paul Crocetti, Joseph Levitch
2. Dean Martin, Steubenville, OH
3. The 500 Club, Atlantic City, NJ
4. The Martin and Lewis Show
5. The Colgate Comedy Hour
6. My Friend Irma (1949)
7. What's My Line?
8. Hollywood or Bust
9. The Copacabana, New York, NY
10. Frank Sinatray

TEST YOUR RECALL • LASSIE, CBS

Answers

PAGE 142

Screen Legends Said

PAGE 143

Fencing

Post 4. A large and a small post always alternate. The number of black posts increases by one from left to right and the number of white posts increases by one from right to left, so it has to be a small white post.

DOODLE PUZZLE • UnEquaLly

PAGE 144

Sport Maze

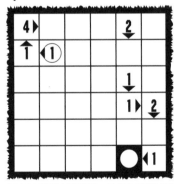

UNCANNY TURN • THE DAWNING

PAGE 145

Presidents Cup—U.S.A.

PAGE 146

Trick or Treat

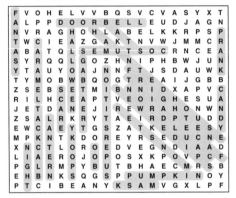

PAGE 147

Sudoku

1	9	7	8	2	5	3	6	4
4	8	6	1	3	7	9	5	2
3	2	5	9	6	4	7	8	1
8	7	2	3	4	1	6	9	5
5	3	9	2	8	6	1	4	7
6	4	1	7	5	9	8	2	3
7	1	8	4	9	2	5	3	6
9	5	4	6	1	3	2	7	8
2	6	3	5	7	8	4	1	9

ONE LETTER LESS OR MORE • DECADES

PAGE 148

Directors Said

PAGE 149

Parks for Grown-ups

1. Denali National Park and Preserve
2. Mammoth Cave National Park
3. Manzanar National Historic Site
4. The completion of the transcontinental railroad
5. Everglades National Park
6. New Mexico
7. Seneca Falls, New York
8. Acadia National Park
9. Great Smoky Mountains National Park
10. Arizona
11. Utah
12. Virginia
13. Texas
14. Wyoming, Montana, and Idaho

PAGE 150

Keep Going

DELETE ONE • DELETE S AND FIND CHANDELIER.

PAGE 151

Presidents Cup— International

A	P	E	R		A	D	L	I	B		A	G	R	A
P	E	R	I		S	H	I	V	A		F	R	O	M
S	A	I	D		C	O	D	E	D		R	E	D	O
E	R	N	I	E	E	L	S		D		A	G	E	S
		C	I	N	E			S	E	T	I	N		
A	B	S	U	R	D		S	A	L	A	D	O	I	L
M	A	C	L	E		O	P	T	E	D		R	N	A
A	C	H	E		I	N	L	A	Y		S	M	U	G
S	O	W		A	S	I	A	N		B	L	A	R	E
S	N	A	P	S	H	O	T		R	E	I	N	E	R
		R	O	S	I	N		B	A	L	M			
M	I	T	T		K		J	A	S	O	N	D	A	Y
O	O	Z	E		A	S	A	B	C		E	U	R	O
O	W	E	N		W	O	N	K	A		S	P	E	W
S	A	L	T		A	D	E	A	L		S	E	A	L

PAGE 152

Honey Cell

Cell 26. Starting from the left and in pairs of columns, columns 1 and 2 each have 1 empty cell; columns 3 and 4 each have 2 empty cells; columns 5 and 6 each have 3 empty cells; columns 7 and 8 each have 4 empty cells; and columns 9 and 10 should each have 5 empty cells.

TRANSADDITION • ADD S AND FIND "CAREFUL FIRST"

PAGE 153

Binairo

I	O	I	I	O	I	O	I	O	O	I
O	I	I	O	O	I	O	I	I	O	I
I	O	O	I	I	O	I	O	I	I	O
O	I	I	O	I	I	O	I	O	I	O
I	I	O	I	O	O	I	O	I	O	I
O	O	I	O	I	O	I	I	O	I	O
O	I	O	I	O	I	I	O	I	I	O
I	O	I	O	O	I	I	O	O	I	I
O	I	I	O	I	O	O	I	I	O	I
I	I	O	I	I	O	I	O	O	I	O
I	O	O	I	O	I	I	O	I	I	O

SANDWICH • COACH

PAGE 154

Webster Says Not 1

T	R	A	P		S	P	R	A	T		H	A	T	S
W	A	R	E		T	E	A	C	H		A	R	A	L
I	R	E	D		R	E	N	E	E		R	A	L	E
G	E	N	E	R	A	L	A	S	S	E	M	B	L	Y
S	E	A	S	O	N	S		T	O	E				
			T	A	D		M	E	A	N	D	E	R	S
M	O	L	A	R		T	E	R	N	S		N	E	E
A	N	I	L		H	E	A	R	D		S	Y	N	E
R	E	O		H	U	R	T	S		T	W	A	I	N
G	I	N	R	U	M	M	Y		P	O	E			
		E	G	O			L	A	V	E	R	N	E	
H	I	G	H	E	R	E	D	U	C	A	T	I	O	N
E	L	I	A		O	S	A	G	E		E	L	L	A
L	E	S	S		U	T	T	E	R		S	E	A	T
P	A	T	H		S	E	E	R	S		T	Y	N	E

PAGE 155

Storied Creatures

1. **a.** Dog
2. **d.** Rabbits
3. **a.** Hedgehog
4. **c.** March hare
5. **d.** Donkey
6. **a.** A little lamb
7. **c.** Polynesia
8. **b.** The lion
9. **a.** Nana
10. **d.** A bear

PAGE 156

Number Cluster

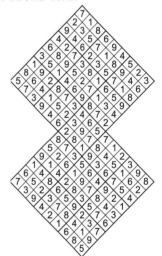

FRIENDS • EACH CAN ADD THE SUFFIX -SHIP TO FORM A NEW WORD.

PAGE 157

Social Contact

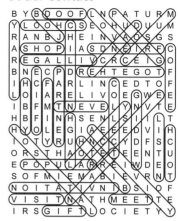

By nature, human beings are inclined to live with sensitivity for the needs of members of their society.

PAGE 158

Sudoku Twin

By nature, human beings are inclined to live with sensitivity for the needs of members of their society.

DOUBLE TALK • FLAIR/FLARE

Answers

PAGE 159

Webster Say Not 2

R	A	N	C	H		L	E	A	R		M	R	E	D
O	M	A	H	A		O	R	L	E		A	H	S	O
T	A	P	I	R		W	I	L	D		R	E	A	L
C	H	A	N	N	E	L	S		E	N	T	A	I	L
			E	E	L	Y		L	E	A	H			
A	G	A	S	S	I		L	A	M	B	A	S	T	E
L	A	N	E	S		F	A	K	E		S	W	A	B
O	T	I	C		L	I	N	E	R		V	A	N	S
N	O	S	H		I	N	K	S		B	I	N	G	E
G	R	E	E	N	B	A	Y		L	E	N	N	O	N
			C	A	R	L		P	E	L	E			
Y	A	N	K	E	E		S	U	K	I	Y	A	K	I
O	N	C	E		T	H	O	R		N	A	R	I	S
G	N	A	R		T	O	T	E		D	R	A	W	N
I	S	A	S		O	I	S	E		A	D	M	I	T

PAGE 160

Cookies

Cookie 3. All connections always depart from a pink icing cookie.

DOODLE PUZZLE • BreakFast

PAGE 161

Word Sudoku

E	N	D	X	T	L	V	S	I
V	X	I	S	E	D	L	N	T
L	S	T	N	V	I	X	E	D
D	T	S	E	L	X	N	I	V
I	E	X	V	N	T	D	L	S
N	V	L	I	D	S	E	T	X
S	L	E	T	X	V	I	D	N
X	I	N	D	S	E	T	V	L
T	D	V	L	I	N	S	X	E

LETTERBLOCKS • WARHOL / CHAGALL

PAGE 162

Big Words 2

R	S	V	P		S	A	T	E	D		A	S	A	P
A	P	E	R		M	I	A	M	I		C	A	B	O
S	C	I	A	P	O	D	O	U	S		O	X	E	N
P	A	N	C	A	K	E	S		P	E	R	I	L	S
			T	I	E	D		F	R	A	N	C		
R	E	M	I	N	D		B	L	O	S	S	O	M	S
E	R	U	C	T		C	R	A	V	E		L	A	T
T	I	L	E		O	R	A	T	E		H	O	P	E
C	C	L		A	V	A	S	T		P	A	U	L	A
H	A	I	R	L	E	S	S		L	E	N	S	E	D
			G	E	A	R	S		L	O	R	D		
G	A	R	L	I	C		S	O	F	T	S	O	A	P
A	L	U	I		O	C	T	O	T	H	O	R	P	E
R	O	B	S		M	O	O	S	E		M	E	A	T
R	U	S	H		E	E	L	E	D		E	L	L	A

PAGE 163

Olives

ABB. For A there is one olive, for B there are two, for C three and for D four. With ABB all possible combinations of groups of two kinds of olives are formed: 1A2B, 1A3C, 1A4D, 2B3C, 2B4D, 3C4D.

REPOSITION PREPOSITION • IN PLACE OF

PAGE 164

History Tour

Castle 6. The historian is only interested in water fortresses.

DOODLE PUZZLE • GrAnt

PAGE 165

Misued?

1. pallet—[C] makeshift bed or portable platform. The roof of the mouth is *palate*; a painter's board is *palette*.

2. sophomoric—[B] immature. People often forget the o in the middle, which can go unpronounced.

3. secede—[B] withdraw. To achieve a goal, and to follow after, is *succeed*.

4. accede—[B] agree. One accedes to a demand but exceeds one's goals.

5. jalousie—[A] window blind. It's related to *jealousy* ("envy") because of people peeking into others' affairs.

6. prevalent—[A] widespread. The tendency to misspell it as *prevalant* is indeed widespread.

7. imminent—[B] about to happen. It's often confused with *eminent* ("outstanding or prominent").

8. aural—[A] of the ears. For mouths, it would be oral; for lights, it would be *auroral*.

9. collegial—[C] marked by camaraderie among colleagues. Its spelling is close to *collegiate* ("relating to a college"), but the meanings are distinct.

10. bellwether—[A] trend leader. This has nothing to do with weather. A *wether* is a sheep, which may wear a bell when leading the flock.

11. climactic—[C] at a decisive moment. It pertains to *climax*, not *climate*, whose adjective is *climatic*.

12. impetus—[B] force, impulse, or stimulus. Don't confuse it with *impotence*, a male sexual dysfunction.

13. emigrate—[A] leave one's residence or country. You emigrate from a country but immigrate to one.

14. incredulous—[B] skeptical. People sometimes mistake this for *incredible*.

15. venial—[B] unimportant. It's no trivial sin to be corrupt and bribable, which is *venal*.

VOCABULARY RATINGS

9 and below: Grammar student
10–12: Junior editor
13–15: Copy chief

PAGE 166
Weigh It Up

It's impossible to weigh 4 grams correctly using only one weighing. All the other weights are possible. For 1, 2 and 8 grams you can use the weights on one side of the scale. You weight the other grams as follows: 3 g = 1 + 2, 5 g + 1 + 2 = 8, 6 g + 2 = 8, 7 g + 1 = 8, 9 g = 8 + 1, 10 g = 8 + 2.

TRANSADDITION • ADD S AND FIND "MAN USES METER"

PAGE 167
Celebrity Chuckles

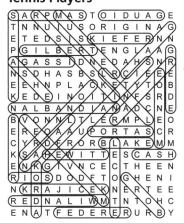

PAGE 168
Tennis Players

Tennis originated in England and has been played in its contemporary form since the end of the nineteenth century.

PAGE 169
Sudoku

5	2	9	6	1	3	8	7	4
3	8	7	9	4	2	6	1	5
1	6	4	8	7	5	3	2	9
6	1	5	4	8	7	2	9	3
9	4	2	3	5	6	7	8	1
7	3	8	2	9	1	5	4	6
8	7	3	1	6	9	4	5	2
4	9	6	5	2	8	1	3	7
2	5	1	7	3	4	9	6	8

ONE LETTER LESS OR MORE • MISPLACED

PAGE 170
Nobility

PAGE 171
Spot the Differences

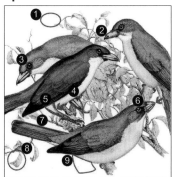

PAGE 172
Symbolism

Symbol 4. Every next figure equals the previous figure where the last piece is a horizontal mirror image and a new piece is added.

DOODLE PUZZLE • ThinKing

PAGE 173
Funny Ladies

Answers

PAGE 174

Keep Going

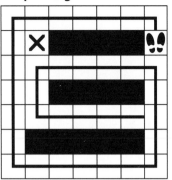

CHANGE ONE • CLOUD NINE

PAGE 175

Winning Colors

1. **a.** Croquet
2. **c.** Toronto
3. **a.** Sunderland
4. **b.** Black
5. **c.** Gold
6. **b.** Black
7. **a.** Red Marauder
8. **a.** Blue
9. **b.** Red
10. **a.** Black
11. **c.** Red
12. **a.** Red

PAGE 176

Themeless

M	A	W	R		S	C	A	M	P		I	C	A	N
A	G	R	O		A	L	A	M	O		R	O	N	A
S	H	E	A		L	U	G	E	R		O	M	N	I
H	A	N	D	S	O	M	E		P	E	N	P	A	L
			S	H	O	P		T	O	S	I	R		
A	C	T	I	O	N		R	A	I	N	C	O	A	T
N	A	R	D	O		G	O	R	S	E		M	A	E
I	R	A	E		W	R	O	T	E		F	I	R	E
T	O	N		C	H	E	S	S		A	R	S	O	N
A	B	S	T	R	A	C	T		A	L	I	E	N	S
		P	H	O	T	O		F	R	A	T			
C	H	O	I	C	E		E	I	N	S	T	E	I	N
H	E	R	R		V	E	R	N	E		E	R	B	E
O	R	T	S		E	R	I	E	S		R	O	A	N
P	E	S	T		R	A	N	D	S		S	O	R	E

PAGE 177

Futoshiki

1	5	2	4	3
2	3	5	1	4
4	1	3 > 2	5
3 < 4	1	5	2
5	2 < 4	3 > 1

CONNECT TWO •
ANXIOUS _____ PATIENT
JUMBO _____ SHRIMP
LIGHT _____ SHADE
AUTO _____ PILOT

PAGE 178

Football Greats

1. **c.** Terry Bradshaw
2. **b.** O. J. Simpson
3. **a.** Dave Casper
4. **b.** Dick Butkus
5. **a.** Merlin Olsen
6. **a.** Jimmy Johnson
7. **a.** Edgerrin James
8. **c.** Peyton Manning
9. **c.** Donovan McNabb
10. **b.** Jeff Garcia

PAGE 179

Kissing Cousins

Number 1	Number 2
1. b	1. f
2. h	2. j
3. j	3. h
4. i	4. b
5. g	5. c
6. d	6. i
7. e	7. a
8. a	8. d
9. f	9. e
10. c	10. g

PAGE 180

MLB Mascots

A	T	O	N		C	O	D	E	D		S	N	O	B
R	E	D	O		A	B	O	V	E		C	A	T	E
A	L	I	T		T	E	N	E	T		A	T	I	T
B	L	U	E	J	A	Y	S		R	E	L	I	S	H
S	Y	M	B	O	L	S		H	A	R	P	O		
			O	N	O		M	I	C	A		N	B	A
R	I	C	O		G	I	A	N	T	S		A	O	L
S	N	A	K	E		R	U	G		E	L	L	I	E
V	C	R		S	P	A	D	E	S		I	S	L	E
P	H	D		T	E	T	E		T	D	S			
	I	S	E	R	E		R	E	D	T	A	P	E	
D	A	N	I	S	H		W	H	I	T	E	S	O	X
E	G	A	N		A	M	A	I	N		N	I	L	E
L	U	L	U		P	A	I	N	E		E	D	E	R
L	A	S	S		S	A	L	E	M		R	E	S	T

PAGE 181

Public Transportation

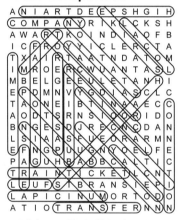

A rickshaw, a kind of bicycle taxi, and a mountable animal can be considered as a form of public transportation.

Sudoku

2	6	7	9	1	8	5	3	4
1	5	4	7	3	6	2	9	8
9	8	3	2	5	4	6	7	1
4	9	2	8	7	5	1	6	3
3	1	5	4	6	9	8	2	7
8	7	6	1	2	3	4	5	9
6	3	9	5	8	1	7	4	2
5	2	8	3	4	7	9	1	6
7	4	1	6	9	2	3	8	5

ONE LETTER LESS OR MORE •
BOREDOM

Capital Namesakes

R	O	T	C		V	R	O	O	M		A	G	E	R
A	E	R	O		I	N	F	R	A		T	O	D	O
I	N	O	N		E	A	T	E	R		H	A	I	M
L	O	N	D	O	N		S	V	E	L	T	E		
			E	N	N	A		T	H	A	N			
	P	E	N	M	A	N		W	A	R	S	A	W	
F	A	L	S	E		G	A	I	L	Y		H	O	W
T	R	E	E		O	U	S	T	S		W	E	R	E
D	I	N		A	L	I	S	T		O	H	A	R	E
	S	I	D	L	E	S		E	M	B	O	D	Y	
		U	T	A	H		R	O	I	L				
L	I	S	B	O	N		S	T	E	V	E	N		
O	R	A	L		D	E	S	A	C		H	A	L	O
L	E	V	I		E	R	A	T	O		O	I	L	S
A	D	E	N		R	E	N	E	W		G	L	E	E

Americana

1. pompadour—[C] men's hairstyle. The piled-up-in-front do, notably worn by Elvis, was named for France's Madame de Pompadour (1721–1764).

2. El Capitan—[B] Yosemite rock formation. It's Spanish for "the captain"—appropriate, since the landmark impressed early explorers as the dominant rock in the valley.

3. jackalope—[A] rabbit with antlers. In Wild West folklore, it's a cross between a jackrabbit and an antelope.

4. barnstorm—[A] travel around performing. Semipro baseball teams used to tour the country playing exhibition games in their off-season.

5. ponderosa—[B] pine tree. The name of this heavy western North American tree has roots (pun intended) in the word ponderous.

6. fake book—[C] collection of songs. Used by jazz and other musicians to quickly learn songs, it has bare-bones melody lines and chord names.

7. tricorn—[C] like Paul Revere's hat. A tricorn hat is bent at three points (tri for "three" plus corn for "corner").

8. bunting—[A] fabric for flags. Made of worsted wool, it is typically used for Fourth of July banners.

9. Tin Pan Alley—[C] pop music center formed in the late 19th century. It was named for the tinkling pianos in a neighborhood of Manhattan songwriters.

10. twain—[C] two. Where the Mississippi River measured two fathoms in depth, steamship workers would call out, "Mark twain!" (hence the pen name of Samuel Clemens).

11. moxie—[B] courage. The word dates back to a soft drink in the 1800s.

12. brushback—[B] baseball pitch. It forces a batter to step back and breaks his confidence.

13. eighty-six—[B] get rid of. Rhyming with nix, it was originally diner slang meaning "to cancel."

14. copacetic—[A] very satisfactory. Its roots are unknown, but tap dancer Bill "Bojangles" Robinson claimed to have invented the word.

VOCABULARY RATINGS
9 and below: Proud
10–12: Patriotic
13–15: All-American

Sunny

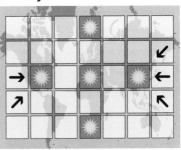

BLOCK ANAGRAM • STATE TROOPER

Word Sudoku

E	H	L	U	P	I	R	M	S
I	U	M	L	R	S	P	H	E
R	S	P	M	H	E	L	U	I
U	R	I	H	S	L	M	E	P
M	L	H	I	E	P	S	R	U
P	E	S	R	U	M	H	I	L
S	M	R	E	L	U	I	P	H
L	I	E	P	M	H	U	S	R
H	P	U	S	I	R	E	L	M

LETTERBLOCKS • OREGANO / PAPRIKA

Crooners

S	N	A	G		A	D	L	I	B	S		B	E	G
I	O	N	E		G	U	I	T	A	R		O	V	A
T	O	N	Y	B	E	N	N	E	T	T		B	I	T
E	R	A	S	E		E	M	O		A	B	L	E	
			E	R	O	S		S	N	O	W	Y		
U	M	B	R	E	L	L	A		S	P	A	D	E	R
T	A	I		T	A	U	P	E		P	R	A	D	O
U	R	N	S		F	R	A	N	K		D	R	U	G
R	I	G	H	T		P	R	U	N	E		I	C	E
N	A	C	R	E	S		T	R	A	W	L	N	E	T
		R	E	N	E	E		E	R	I	E			
G	O	O	D		P	S	I			N	E	W	E	R
I	D	S		N	A	T	K	I	N	G	C	O	L	E
F	O	B		S	L	E	E	V	E		T	R	A	P
T	R	Y		A	S	S	A	Y	S		Y	E	N	S

PAGE 188

Word Wheel

ask, back, bake, bask, beak, cake, sack, take, task, teak, skate, stack, stake, steak, basket, casket, backseat, backstage

PAGE 189

Shipping

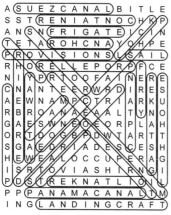

A bit less than ninety percent of international world trade occurs via shipping.

PAGE 190

The Play's the Thing

L	O	G	O		A	G	A	M	A		P	H	I	L
E	C	R	U		R	A	Y	O	N		S	E	L	A
T	H	E	T	E	M	P	E	S	T		E	N	I	D
T	R	E	L	L	I	S		S	E	C	U	R	E	D
S	E	N	I	L	E			L	A	D	Y			
		N	I	S	I		D	O	N	O	V	A	N	
F	A	C	E	S		D	R	I	P	S		I	P	O
L	A	Y	S		E	L	I	T	E		P	I	E	D
A	R	M		O	L	E	O	S		V	O	I	D	S
W	E	B	S	T	E	R		Y	E	A	R			
		E	P	I	C				S	P	R	I	N	G
C	A	L	I	S	T	A		S	T	O	I	C	A	L
O	V	I	D		R	I	C	H	A	R	D	I	I	I
P	I	N	E		I	D	I	O	T		G	E	L	D
E	V	E	R		C	A	S	T	E		E	R	S	E

PAGE 191

Train Your Brain

Jumping for Joy

D is the missing figure

Find the Flag

C is the missing figure

PAGE 192

Sudoku X

2	8	4	1	6	9	5	7	3
7	9	5	2	3	4	1	6	8
6	3	1	8	7	5	4	9	2
9	5	6	3	4	8	2	1	7
8	1	3	7	5	2	9	4	6
4	2	7	9	1	6	8	3	5
3	4	2	6	8	1	7	5	9
5	7	9	4	2	3	6	8	1
1	6	8	5	9	7	3	2	4

LETTERLINE • KINGFISHER; GRIEF, HINGE, FRISK, FEIGN

PAGE 193

Sport Maze

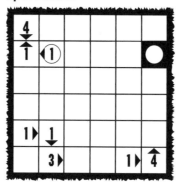

UNCANNY TURN • FAMILY TREE

PAGE 194

Choose Your Cheese

Cheese cube 3. The mouse chooses the cheese cubes with the fewest number of holes. It already collected the cubes with 0, 1, 2 and 3 holes. The cube with four holes is the next one.

REPOSITION PREPOSITION • ASIDE / FROM

PAGE 195

Weather-Wise

A	L	E	C		S	C	R	U	B		E	D	N	A
M	I	L	O		Q	U	A	K	E		N	E	E	D
A	K	I	N		U	R	G	E	D		O	G	E	E
H	E	A	T	W	A	V	E	S		P	U	R	R	S
			E	I	R	E			D	O	G	E		
H	A	S	S	L	E		N	O	R	T	H	E	R	N
A	C	U	T	E		B	O	N	U	S		D	O	O
R	A	P	S		F	L	A	T	T		P	A	Y	E	E
S	S	E		F	L	A	T	T		P	A	Y	E	E
H	E	R	M	I	O	N	E		K	R	I	S	T	Y
		C	A	V	E			C	O	O	L			
S	H	E	R	E		C	O	L	D	F	R	O	N	T
H	E	L	M		H	A	N	O	I		O	S	A	R
O	R	L	O		A	R	E	N	A		A	L	T	A
P	A	S	T		D	E	R	E	K		D	O	O	M

PAGE 196

Kakuro

4	5	2		1	3	5		7
8		5	4	7	6		9	5
	3	7	8		7	2	1	8
5	2	6			9	6		9
6		8	4	2		1	2	3
9	1		2	6	7		7	
	5	1		6		1	8	
9	3	8	6	2		9	5	
3	2		2	1		4	3	2

MISSING LETTER PROVERB • THE MORE THE MERRIER.

Architecture & Construction

1. raze—[C] tear down. I hear they're going to *raze* the mall and build a greenhouse.

2. dexterous—[A] skillful. Charlotte spun her web with amazingly *dexterous* eight-handedness.

3. jury-rig—[B] construct in a make-shift fashion. The contractors were let go after they *jury-rigged* our home's first floor.

4. stud—[C] upright post. Don't start hammering the wall until you locate a *stud* behind it.

5. on spec—[B] without a contract. Dad is building the girls' dollhouse *on spec*.

6. garret—[A] attic room. I'm not fancy—a cozy garret is all I need to finish the novel.

7. annex—[A] supplementary structure. The children's *annex* was a welcome
addition to the library.

8. wainscot—[C] paneled part of a wall. Marge's kids have treated the entire *wainscot* as an experimental crayon mural.

9. rotunda—[B] circular room. The conflicting blueprints for the *rotunda* have me going in circles!

10. plumb—[C] vertical. Our fixer-up-per may need new floors, doors, and windows, but at least the walls are *plumb*.

11. aviary—[A] house for birds. "Your cat hasn't taken his eyes off that *aviary*," Sheryl noted.

12. corrugated—[C] having a wavy surface. All we have for a roof is a sheet of *corrugated* tin.

13. mezzanine—[A] lowest balcony floor. Sadly, our $165 seats in the *mezzanine* had an obstructed view.

14. cornice—[B] decorative top edge. You're going to need one heck of an extension ladder to reach that cornice.

15. vestibule—[B] lobby. Anxiety peaking, Claire waited over an hour in the *vestibule* for her interview.

VOCABULARY RATINGS
9 and below: Homey
10–12: Grand
13–15: Palatial

Fall Traditions

M	O	T	E	L		H	A	S		A	H	A
A	L	I	C	E		A	L	I		G	A	L
T	E	S	L	A		H	A	R	V	E	S	T
		A	R	E	A	S		I	N	T	O	
R	A	K	I	N	G			H	A	T	E	S
A	V	E	R		R	A	R	E				
H	A	G		D	E	T	E	R		P	I	E
		I	T	E	M		O	H	N	O		
R	A	T	E	D		I	N	D	I	A	N	
I	B	I	S		V	I	T	A	E			
P	U	M	P	K	I	N		P	S	A	L	M
E	S	E		E	L	K		E	S	T	E	E
R	E	D		Y	E	S		S	A	L	O	N

Loop the Loops

1. The yellow pieces make a complete loop.

2. The blue pieces make a complete loop.

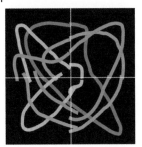

Answers

p. 9: Blood

p. 16: 4

p. 17: Cast

p. 18: Light

p. 21: Albert Einstein

p. 24: The Sun

p. 32: Snoopy

p. 38: In your throat

p. 40: C

p. 45: Small, steamed cakes made with masa, or ground corn

p. 51: Someone who won't eat any food of animal origin

p. 54: Tallahassee

p. 61: In the eye

p. 66: Cardiac arrest

p. 67: Calla Lily

p. 69: Arthur Hailey

p. 70: Five

p. 81: Eva Perón in *Evita*

p. 85: Ethiopia

p. 89: Argentina national football team

p. 99: A French cheese

p. 102: Sydney, Australia

p. 103: In the knee

p. 105: Frank Gehry

p. 110: Tomato

p. 111: J. M. Barrie

p. 112: Charles Lindbergh

p. 118: *Thunderball*

p. 119: The Mad Hatter, the March Hare, the Dormouse and Alice

p. 121: Serena

p. 124: The branch of knowledge concerned with medicinal drugs obtained from plants or other natural sources

p. 128: Charolette Bronte's *Jane Eyre*

p. 134: *The Comedy of Errors* (Act III, Scene ii)

p 137: Benny Goodman

p. 144: 33 bones—7 vertebrae in the cervical region, 12 in the thoracic region, 5 in the lumbar region, 5 in the sacral region and 4 in the coccygeal region

p. 147: Petals

p. 153: Bumblebee

p. 156: Andy Gibb

p. 161: Piano

p. 169: Paris

p. 171: Pablo

p. 182: Vitamin C

p. 186: Dead Sea

p. 192: Venezuela

p. 193: Sound effects

p. 196: The Andes

p. 199: Plum tree

p. 18: Kenneth "Ken" Sean Carson

p. 41: China

p. 63: "Kolf" or "kolve"

p. 66: Ahab

p. 84: The *Jolly Roger*

p. 119: Pennsylvania Dutch

p. 125: 8 minutes, 20 seconds

p. 130: Bobby Fischer

p. 136: Poopeye, Peepeye, Pupeye and Pipeye

p. 171: Six legs

p. 177: Ginger

p. 188: Kim Carnes

p. 199: George Clooney

CREDITS

Cover photo credit:
ziviani/Shutterstock

Puzzle credits:
Peter Frank: Binairo, Kakuro, Number Cluster, Sudoku, Word Searches, Word Sudoku

David Bodycombe: 132, 133, 199

Brainwarp: 23, 92

Guy Campell and Paul Moran: 15, 191

Ken Russell and Philip Carter: 43, 93

Emily Cox & Henry Rathvon: 20, 64, 165, 184, 197

Don Law: 22, 129

Kelly Lynch: 100, 123, 135, 167

John McCarthy: 11

Peggy O'Shea: 29, 36, 138, 170

Karen Peterson: 14, 42, 68, 71, 176

John M. Samson: 19, 47, 56, 97, 113, 114, 126, 142, 148, 154, 159, 162, 183, 190, 195

Michele Sayer: 8, 50, 78, 83, 86, 95, 180

Justin Scroggie: 48

Debra Steilen: 46, 77, 96, 130, 141

Tim Wagner: 53, 59, 145, 151

Cindy Wheeler: 62, 117, 120

Kelly Whitt: 26, 33, 39, 73, 91, 106, 109, 173, 187, 198